ONLY THE BEST

Only The Best

Summaries and Evaluations
of Today's Top
Twenty Business Books

Editor
Jagdish N. Sheth

Reviews Editor
Glenn Morrison

Business Book Review

Champaign, Illinois

Cover Design: Roxanne Walker
Production Coordinator: Publication Services

ISBN 0–936879–00–9

Contents

Introduction

Only the Best is a collection of reviews of excellent books representing the top of the pyramid, the final product of a long, tough screening process. Throughout the year we scan virtually all business books marketed in the United States to select those that promise the greatest value for time-pressed executives and managers. The few that are chosen are further scrutinized and analyzed until only the best remain.

Six times a year **Business Book Review** evaluates and summarizes ten of these best books offering management ideas from the experts, biographies of top corporations and CEOs, information on special business topics, professional references, and advice for personal and career enrichment. This book, **Only the Best**, contains our pick of the top twenty books—the best of the best.

These twenty reviews selected from past issues are designed to give you a clear picture of what we believe to be the most important books for business professionals. For ready reference, each review begins with a *capsule* that provides a short evaluation, sets out the book's thesis, identifies the intended audience, and estimates reading time.

The review proper opens with a description of the *author's background*, experience, and point of view. The *audience and intentions* section that follows analyzes the book's assumptions, purposes, and targeted readers. Next, chapter by chapter *summaries* detail the essential contents and ideas.

The extended *evaluation* discusses the presentational qualities of style, development, and readability before examining the worth of the book's argument, character of information, and practical value to the business professional.

After the evaluation we suggest strategies readers might employ to get the most out of the book in the least amount of time. Complete ordering information, including price, concludes the review.

We hope our book will benefit you the same way **Business Book Review** benefits its subscribers: (1) by saving critical search and reading time and (2) by locating and evaluating sources of vital information. We think business people need and deserve only the best.

Jagdish N. Sheth, Editor
Glenn Morrison, Reviews Editor
Champaign, Illinois February 1986

A Passion for Excellence: The Leadership Difference

Tom Peters and Nancy Austin

Random House

© 1985
437 pages

Evaluation: A work of considerable energy and conviction that attempts to provide the motivation and practical guidance necessary to work toward excellence. The book is an exhaustive compilation of opinions, stories, and advice.

Thesis: Excellence is attained by serving customers well, providing high quality products, constantly innovating, offering strong leadership through attention to details, and treating people with respect—all with enthusiasm and intensity.

Audience: Especially for top executives who can set the tone of an organization; also for all managers who want to create a "pocket" of excellence.

Reading Time: 12 to 14 hours.

Authors

Tom Peters was a partner at McKinsey & Co. when he and Robert H. Waterman, Jr. wrote *In Search of Excellence* (1982). He has since formed a group of companies involved in consulting and publishing. Peters continues to write and lecture.

Nancy Austin is president of Not Just Another Publishing Company, a member of the Tom Peters Group. Formerly she conducted management development seminars at Hewlett-Packard. Austin is the author, with Stanlee Phelps, of *The Assertive Woman*.

Audience and Intentions

Peters and Austin contend that (1) there is a "back to basics" revolution going on in management in response to the perceived failure of complex "techniques, devices, and programs"; (2) *In Search of Excellence* (hereafter *Search*) and a few other volumes have attempted to turn the dissatisfaction toward a reemphasis on concern for people (workers and consumers); (3) despite the enormous commercial success of *Search*, its tenets are imperfectly understood—because it was not simple enough, or enthusiastic enough, for most readers to put into operation; and (4) after hundreds of seminars and lectures the authors are convinced that more help is needed.

A Passion for Excellence (hereafter **Passion**) responds to that need. The new book is designed to be the first step in learning how to practice excellence. "It is an avowed Whitman's Sampler of the passion for excellence observed and celebrated." The authors hope it will give people "heart as well as practical, straightforward guidance."

"Heart" is necessary because passion/spirit/energy is a vital ingredient in an organization's success. Spirit comes from a leadership style that embraces the tough-tender paradox. Peters and Austin say that the best bosses are "tough on the values, tender in support of people who would dare to take a risk and try something new in support of those values."

"Practical, straightforward guidance" is also required because good leaders must "delve unmercifully into the details." The book offers numerous "deep-penetrating" examples to capture "the smell" of "hard-nosed, bottom-line oriented management": that is, serving customers well, providing superior-quality products, and constantly innovating.

Since **Passion** is about leadership and setting the tone, its obvious focus is on CEOs and top management. Peters and Austin assert, however, that their book is also for "first-line supervisors" and for those "who run garages and corner stores." They believe that excellence, as they define it, is possible at every level.

Summary

Part I: Common Sense

Chapter 1: A Blinding Flash of the Obvious (5 pages)

The lessons from *Search* were obvious, but not always seen; the advice was common sense, but not very common. To create and sustain superior performance (1) take care of your customers with superior service and quality, (2) constantly innovate, (3) turn on your people by listening and giving them respect, (4) provide leadership by consistently displaying an obsession with key values, and (5) stay in touch with all variables so that your organization can be adaptive.

Chapter 2: MBWA: The Technology of the Obvious (26 pages)

The number one managerial productivity problem is being out of touch with employees and with customers. The solution is MBWA: Managing By Wandering Around. It means "naive" listening to customers, that is, considering their perceptions more important than your superior technical knowledge of your service or product. Customers are always delighted by the attention. Call a minimum of three customers per week; make sure you talk to bad and indifferent as well as good customers. Set up an 800 number, invite customers to visit, and have senior managers work in customer operations on a regular basis.

MBWA is also essential for innovation because it forces management to pay attention to innovation and experimentation on a daily basis. The sales force and the customers are good—and neglected—sources for new ideas. Set up a regular mechanism for mining this vein of innovation. Finally, the MBWA approach focuses on people: it offers the opportunity to listen, facilitate, and teach.

Chapter 3: Integrity and the Technology of the Obvious (2 pages)

Truly listening to your customers and your people is vital to successful MBWA, but the technique will fail if not applied with integrity. No matter what you preach or what device you try, if you don't treat your customers and people as more important than yourself, your organization will suffer.

Part Two: Customers

Chapter 4: Common Courtesy: The Ultimate Barrier to Competitor Entry (10 pages)

Customer orientation is superior to market orientation because customers, not markets, buy products. You must cherish the customer and be slavishly devoted to adding value and providing superior service and quality.

Many firms practice TDC—thinly disguised contempt—for customers and front-line people actually delivering service. It is manifested in such things as poor phone courtesy and a belief that technological superiority is all that counts. Because those attitudes are invariably handed down to the customer, they are the biggest barrier to sustained superior performance. Excellence is a game of many, many little things that amount to the marginal difference.

Chapter 5: No Such Thing as a Commodity (20 pages)

People who produce for the higher ends of the market tend to be winners over the long haul. They focus on "revenue line enhancement": quality, service, courtesy, customer listening, and problem-solving for tailored market segments. Relative product quality, as perceived by customers, is much more important than relative market share. Quality should be of greater concern than cost.

Companies must offer something that is distinctive if not unique. Never label a product or service a "commodity." Start with quality and achieve low cost as a result, because a low-cost mindset leads to poor quality and service and retards innovation. Starting with quality generates customers; focusing on costs drives them away.

Chapter 6: "Mere Perception": On the Irreducible Humanness of Customers (27 pages)

The way we perceive the value of a service or product is the only reality. It improves customers' perceptions of service if they are made aware that real human beings like themselves are working on their problems. Impersonality is the ultimate discourtesy. The little things matter in repeat business, and they are remembered for a very long time.

Complaints, however, are opportunities to provide special service and make lifetime customers. No complaint is unique; they always signal an iceberg of problems.

Customer satisfaction is always rated as important by managers, but they never measure it for purposes of compensation and evaluation of employees. Customer service must be a top priority, regardless of cost. And it must be defined in the customers' terms.

Chapter 7: Quality Is Not a Technique (9 pages)

Any device to maintain quality can be of value if managers at all levels live the quality message with passion and consistency. They must understand that quality comes from people who care and are committed. For an organization to be truly exceptional, senior management should have "grown up around the product." If you haven't done so, get in touch by MBWA—and trust enthusiasm and pride.

Chapter 8: The "Smell" of the Customer (5 pages)

A true customers-first orientation can be developed, and it must be pursued with obsessive intensity. Customers-first companies have several practices in common: (1) they tell stories about working with customers, (2) they demonstrate respect for salespeople and customer support people, (3) they speak of customers in a friendly manner, and (4) they view the customer's perception as most important.

Part III: Innovation

Chapter 9: The Mythology of Innovation, or a Skunkworks Tale (46 pages)

The course of innovation is very uncertain; it is, however, always messy. Thus it is necessary to follow a model that takes advantage of messiness. The only way to proceed is by constant experimentation under the direction of "champions" ("skunks"). The effective environment for champions of experimentation is an abundance of skunkworks, small decentralized teams operating outside the mainline of the organization. Finally, innovation requires a climate conducive to experiments, champions, and skunkworks.

Managing innovation means exchanging the truth for myths. (1) Forget no-surprises planning; learn to live with uncertainty and ambiguity. (2) Experiment and move fast rather than spend time developing a sound set of specifications. (3) Creativity comes from passion, not intellectual reflection. (4) Small skunkworks are superior to big, formal groups. Link functions together instead of dividing them. (5) Forget that last 2 percent of product compatibility in order to get into and capture the market; optimize later. (6) Give prototypes to lead users to find out what is needed and wanted.

Chapter 10: Three Skunks (8 pages)

Three particularly effective "skunks," or champions of innovation, were Tom West of Data General, Kelly Johnson of Lockheed, and Gerhard Neumann of GE. West invited his people to "sign up" for the duration of a project and then trusted them to accomplish it. Their reward was the chance to work on the most interesting jobs. Kelly organized his teams by choosing the "best" people in each skill and making them want to live up to that assessment. Neumann demonstrated the values of small groups, drama or pizzazz, daily reviews, and MBWA.

Chapter 11: The Context of Innovation (24 pages)

Ordinary people can be turned into vigorous, enthusiastic experimenters by creating the right environment, the context of innovation. Several factors are important: informality, all-hands involvement, a spirit of fun, creation of new divisions, and strong leadership. Open discussions also induce the huge number of rapid tries that are essential for bringing in a constant stream of winners.

It helps to tell stories of past innovations: how people cheated the system and succeeded. Make heroes of your rule breakers. You also have to talk freely about past failures to let people know it's OK to fail if they make a *good* try.

Skunkworks must be physically separate from the main business, but not too distant, to create a sense of team spirit. Spartan, open quarters help too. You also need enough of them to guarantee the number of tries needed to succeed.

Chapter 12: The "Smell of Innovation" (4 pages)

Innovative companies exhibit several common characteristics. (1) They do not tolerate inaction. (2) They constantly test and experiment. (3) They learn from failures. (4) Eccentricity is acceptable as long as it doesn't interfere with practical teamwork. (5) Physical layout encourages informal communication. (6) Management tells both success and failure stories about innovation and skunkworks operations. There are many more, as well.

Part IV: People, People, People

Chapter 13: Bone-Deep Beliefs (10 pages)

Many managers betray their thinly disguised contempt for their people in their minute-to-minute behavior and in their language. In contrast, excellent companies assume that all people are capable of caring and contributing if management cares for and believes in them. Employees bring their own motivation; they need to be involved and to be accountable if they are to reach their potential.

The little slights—like executive washrooms and parking places—kill the spirit. Respect for people demands presence, visiting the plant, MBWA. You can't lose your dignity if you are confident in your beliefs and live them with integrity.

Chapter 14: Ownership! (39 pages)

Excellence results from making everybody part of the strategic information stream of the business, making everybody an owner. People who are part of the team, who "own" their job, regularly perform a thousand percent better. Treat all people as business people and they become committed to the business's success. Ownership enhances pride in ourselves and in our associates. It engenders enthusiasm. Recognition and respect make valued experts of routine performers.

The process of giving people responsibility or ownership demands integrity and guts from leadership. Managers who believe in the capacity of people give honest recognition and opportunity. They have the courage to surrender control and to resist the impulse to step into a situation and thus deny their people the chance of a fair effort.

Giving people ownership means giving people space, and that is possible only in small organizational units. Create small teams of 10 to 20 members. But remember that they work only if leaders believe in them and don't undercut them with rules. Persistence pays off, and management eventually gets the work force—good or bad—it deserves.

Chapter 15: ApplauseApplause (10 pages)

Winners are people who have fun, and they produce as a result of their zest. There is no limit to the possibilities for large and small celebrations; weekly hoopla is very good for morale. Develop programs that boost the enthusiasm of your organization just as systematically as you would develop a new product or process. Be sure to include secretaries and other support staff. Awards, however, must be given with conviction and for merit; integrity, as always, is vital.

Part V: Leadership

Chapter 16: Attention, Symbols, Drama, Vision—and Love
(29 pages)

All business is show business. Leadership means shaping values, being enthusiastic, nurturing champions, finding heroes, wandering throughout the organization, coaching, and facilitating. It involves passion, care, intensity, consistency, attention, drama, and the implicit and explicit use of symbols.

People pay attention to the obsessions of managers. They notice who gets promoted; they are alert when actions don't match the speeches. Attention is symbolic behavior, driven home by consistency and many repetitions. Dramatic actions make for good stories whose lessons are remembered and retold for years.

Leaders must be able to state their visions for their organizations clearly and concisely—and care about them passionately. Visions should be realistic and should stress the positive. Leaders pay equal attention to ideals and the details of execution. By caring they encourage others in their organization to do the same.

Chapter 17: Transformations and Enhancements: Small Wins, Debureaucratizing and Pockets of Excellence
(30 pages)

Moving toward excellence is accomplished by (1) setting up a system for generating a series of small wins and (2) consciously rolling back the excessive regulators and regulations that get in the way of ownership—thus debureaucratizing the organization. The first builds winners and ownership; the second keeps people from becoming losers or disenfranchised.

The small win is do-able, tangible, and fast. Tasks that can be done by average persons are given real-time feedback to increase confidence and involvement. Management must, however, exercise patience to guide people to autonomy. Go after the easy stuff first and let change diffuse naturally throughout the organization.

One response to the need to reduce bureaucracy is to eliminate as many policies and rules as possible. Real control comes when (1) people realize that someone who cares is paying attention and (2) a small number of simple rules is directly consistent with the company's vision. Cut staff numbers and *layers*. If you don't have the authority to eliminate, create your own pocket of excellence and ignore the paperwork.

Chapter 18: Coaching (54 pages)

Leaders must be consistent to be believed: if they say people are special, they must treat them that way—*always*. They demonstrate everyday where they want to take their organization; they make their purpose clear through mundane actions. They pay close attention to their environment and patiently develop their people. High performance leaders are, then, really dedicated, enthusiastic coaches.

The vital aspects of coaching are visibility, listening, limit setting, value shaping, and skill stretching. Coaching involves caring enough about people to build a personal relationship through time and attention. It is trust developed through integrity—when actions are consistent with stated values. Successful coaches vary only their approaches to meet people's changing needs. They perform five different roles: they educate, sponsor, coach, counsel, and confront.

The prime educational message to employees is that they belong and can contribute. As educators, leaders treat all their people as full-fledged team members. The education process is characterized by accountability and unwavering support. It is used to orient newcomers, including managers, and teach new skills, goals, and roles.

The coach as sponsor assumes that key skills are already in place. Sponsors grant practical autonomy by removing obstacles to performance. They treat people as colleagues, regularly discuss career plans and goals, and desperately and passionately want their people to succeed.

Coaching teaches people how to contribute and participate as active, full partners. It means creating winners by building on strengths. It includes praise *and* support—the assertive trust that people will overcome difficulty.

The counseling role leads people to understand and overcome those problems that limit performance. It requires taking time to help at points of crisis. Counseling can *not* be performed without the right or invitation to intervene. When done with care it builds trust. Confronting is a form of counseling in which the alternatives and consequences are clear and close at hand. It is the last ditch role when a company has done all it can to solve a persistent problem.

Chapter 19: Doing MBWA (15 pages)

Leading/coaching is a difficult, time-consuming, hands-on art. It can, however, be learned. Doing MBWA entails three activities: listening, teaching, and facilitating. Listening is getting information first hand, and it is a form of caring. Teaching transmits values face-to-face. Finally, wandering allows the coach/leader to be of direct help, to facilitate the destruction of the bureaucracy.

MBWA is about delegation, the toughest issue in management. Wanderers, in fact, are tough-minded; but they leave their people with space enlarged, not diminished. When MBWA is done honestly and frequently, managers *earn* honest feedback. Any supervisor should be out of the office 50 to 75 percent of the time. And all wanderers must have the integrity to withstand this exposure.

Chapter 20: Excellence in School Leadership (21 pages)

Evidence indicates that the framework for excellence in business can be applied to schools, where leadership is also important and where the "common sense" of treating people (i.e., teachers) as adults is far from common. As with corporations, the best schools are imbued with clear philosophies that are lived with intensity. They are led by good principals who are showmen, visionaries, symbol users, and salesmen. They pay attention to details, including the physical trappings.

Teachers *and* principals practice MBWA. They personalize education by focusing on the customer—the kids. They treat pupils with respect; they care. Principals with a passion for excellence are tough disciplinarians, but they encourage faculty creativity and autonomy. They instill a family feeling in the schools.

Chapter 21: What Price Excellence? (6 pages)

The "adventure" of excellence is not for the faint of heart. You need "tenacious preparation" and a purpose you can care about intensely. It is a task easily begun but never finished. Passion opens you to criticism and disappointment; it means lost sleep and long hours. It does *not* mean no home life, although it probably will create an imbalance between personal and professional selves.

But the rewards of achievement, sense of purpose, and self-respect are worth the price.

* * *

At the conclusion of parts II, III, IV, and V, the authors describe a few books (four to ten volumes) they can recommend on the topics just discussed. The contributions of several executives, colleagues, and publications are noted in the text. Publication information, where relevant, is listed as part of the acknowledgments.

Peters and Austin also provide a two-page listing of key concepts—in their own special terminology—arranged by chapter in the order of presentation (rather than alphabetically). This serves as a subject index. There is also an index for people, companies, and titles.

Evaluation

Presentation

Peters and Austin's tone is friendly and informal, even personal. They are opinionated, direct, simple, emphatic, and repetitious. **Passion** goes beyond *Search* in the thoroughness with which it embodies its authors' beliefs about attaining excellence: it is deliberately—but, we suspect, naturally—"messy," intimate, and enthusiastic.

Form follows function. The book is out to convince us that attention to detail and passion constitute the road to salvation. That accounts both for the revivalist style in which the authors and various practitioners (believers) get up one after another and testify. It also accounts for the insistence on integrity or sincerity—and the presentation of story after story after story.

Peters and Austin believe in practicing what they preach. And they believe in preaching. Sometimes, of course, this means they come to love their message and their metaphors too much: this can make the reading tedious after a while. But the occasional dry patch is more than made up for by the passages that move you to jump up and shout "that's right!"

Content

Peters and Austin are clearly excited about their message and further aroused that, after hundreds of seminars on *Search for Excellence* and millions of books sold, the world is not totally converted—the revolution, as they term it, is not yet well launched. But **A Passion for Excellence** is not, as some cynics might expect, a "Son of *Search for Excellence*." **Passion** is more comprehensive, perhaps because it is based on more data and three full years of feedback on the "lessons" of *Search*. It expounds a coherent philosophy that is more personal, less mechanical, and it is certainly more oriented toward implementation.

There are other messages in **Passion** besides *passion*, because Peters and Austin are not fanatics (obsession, they say, is necessary: being divorced from reality is not). One recurring theme is that excellence does not come easily. The book pauses periodically to remind us that its solution requires hard work, guts, time, and integrity. MBWA is a long, hard road. **Passion** is exhaustive, and exhausting, on purpose: belief rather than the promise of reward is paramount.

Beyond the "bottom-line management" of customer service, quality, and innovation is a definition of leadership that Peters and Austin call the "single most significant message" of **Passion**. It is: "Treat your people like adults, and they will respond as adults, conscientiously and creatively. Treat them with contempt, and they will respond with contempt for you and your product."

Reading Suggestions

You may find your interest and enthusiasm waxing and waning as you make your way through **Passion**. Probably the best approach is to quit when you feel like quitting, but make yourself pick up the task again. **Passion** is a long and demanding work. The authors' advice to give the book hard use by underlining and making notes is well taken. In that respect, reading it is much like applying its teachings.

Ordering Information:	Random House 201 East 50th Street New York, New York 10022
Call:	1 (800) 638-6460
Specify:	ISBN 0-394-54484-6
Price:	$19.95

Iacocca: An Autobiography

Lee Iacocca, with William Novak

Bantam Books

© 1984
352 pages

Evaluation: A quickly paced and highly interesting account of Lee Iacocca's career at Ford and Chrysler. The author also draws some moral and managerial lessons and explains his positions on auto industry and economic issues.

Audience: For a general readership; no real background in business nor passion for cars required.

Reading Time: 7 to 9 hours.

Audience and Intentions

Lee Iacocca says that he had been putting people's curiosity off with "wait until I write my book" for so long that he felt compelled to actually write one. Further, he asserts he did *not* write the book to become famous, make money, or get back at Henry Ford, because he is satisfied on all those accounts. "The truth is," he goes on, "that I wrote this book to set the record straight (and to keep my mind straight)...."

Be advised, however, that the first rule of autobiographies is that every assertion is a little suspect because although the author is an inside source, he is not a disinterested observer. The author's motivations—not just for writing but for all actions—most especially must be taken with at least a pinch of salt.

We are, of course, readily willing to accept the not-in-it-for-the-money motivation since all of Iacocca's royalties are going to the Joslin Diabetes Center. For the others, it is best to recall that "setting the record straight" depends considerably on your perception and so can mean many things.

Another fundamental reason why people write autobiographies is the same as the one given to us in grade school when we had to read the life of George Washington—that is, moral instruction. Authors want to draw some lessons from their lives and pass them on to us. For Lee Iacocca that urge takes two forms. First, he wants to reach the "young people" and paint them "a realistic picture of the excitement and challenge of big business in America today and some idea of what is worth fighting for." Second, for all of us, he wants to tell the story of "something constructive born out of adversity," that is, his story. There will be morals drawn at key points in the narrative.

Content Overview

The book consists of 28 short chapters, organized into four sections, and an epilogue.

Made in America (24 pages, 2 chapters)

Lee Iacocca was born in America in 1924 to parents who had emigrated from Italy 20 years previously. He grew up in Allentown, Pennsylvania during the Great Depression and experienced economic hardship as his father's businesses suffered. He also learned, however, the value of strong family ties and perseverance.

Lee was a good student in high school. An adolescent illness made him 4F, and he was able to attend Lehigh University during World War II. Iacocca earned a degree in engineering and went on to graduate school at Princeton before joining the Ford Motor Company.

The Ford Story (109 pages, 10 chapters)

Iacocca began working at Ford in 1946 as a student engineer. After nine months, he talked his way out of the program and into a sales job with a district office near Philadelphia. Here he worked with Charlie Beacham and developed a respect for the importance of good relationships with the dealers.

Iacocca's phenomenal record with installment sales in 1956 caught the attention of the home office. Newly married, he moved to Dearborn to become national truck marketing manager. Robert McNamara—one of the original Whiz Kids—was a vice-president of the Ford division at the time. McNamara helped discipline Iacocca's thinking and made it easier for him to move up in the company. McNamara had great success with the Falcon, a simple subcompact, and became president of Ford before moving on to become John Kennedy's Secretary of Defense.

Iacocca followed McNamara as head of the Ford Division in 1960 at the age of 36. He instituted a quarterly review system and exhibited the decisiveness and the ability to motivate that are the hallmarks of a good manager. But Lee really established himself when he put together the team that created the Mustang. The Mustang was a more muscular and sportier version of the Falcon, and its introduction rejuvenated sales at Ford. Iacocca followed up on his triumph by energizing the moribund Lincoln-Mercury Division with new quality products.

Nevertheless, in 1968 Iacocca was passed over for president. Instead, Henry Ford gave the job to Bunkie Knudsen, son of the legendary General Motors executive. Bunkie couldn't cut it, however, and by the end of 1970 Iacocca was made president—the number two man behind Henry Ford.

Playing second fiddle to the grandson of the founder proved to be a difficult role. Henry was paranoiac and self-indulgent; he still regarded the company as a family business, although it had gone public years ago. Despite Iacocca's superior record, Henry was never comfortable with the son of an Italian immigrant. After a bizarre period of intrigue that left some bitter feelings and psychological scars, Iacocca was fired during the summer of 1978.

The Chrysler Story (149 pages, 12 chapters)

Suddenly without a company at the age of 54, Iacocca did not want to retire, become a business school dean, or begin again in a new industry. He was thus receptive to overtures from the ailing Chrysler Company. Lee knew little about Chrysler—at Ford they concentrated on GM—except its long-established reputation for engineering excellence. When he took over as president—and soon to be CEO—he discovered an organization in total disarray that was losing money at an incredible rate. Chrysler was long on incompetent managers and short on quality products to sell.

Iacocca's first step was to forge a top-flight management team. As he weeded out the old executives—with more honesty and sensitivity than he had experienced at Ford—he filled the ranks with managers from his old company, retired executives (again from Ford), and juniors from Chrysler whose talents had been lost in the confusion.

Life in the auto business took a drastic turn for the worse, just as Chrysler was gearing up, when the ouster of the Shah from Iran sparked a second oil crisis and the country headed into a long and very severe recession. All American auto companies began losing vast sums of money, but Chrysler was by far in the most precarious condition. Iacocca cut staff positions and reduced costs everywhere to stay afloat. Yet, that still left the problem of new product development: to make the new energy-efficient cars America now demanded, millions had to be spent on production. To get the funds, Chrysler went to the government.

Philosophically, it was a difficult decision, and much of the opposition in Congress was ideological, namely, an aversion to "violating" the free enterprise system. Iacocca went through fire during the many hearings, but he eventually won loan guarantees by pointing out that there was considerable precedent and that thousands of people and the national economy would suffer if Chrysler were to collapse. Congress was also impressed by the steps the company had already taken to become competitive again.

The loan guarantees were actually a very safe investment for the government because they held a lien on all the company's assets, which could have been liquidated for more money than had been lent. Congress also stipulated that all of Chrysler's over 400 lenders approve the agreement. This turned out to be an intricate and exhausting task, perhaps only made possible by the monetary sacrifices made by both Chrysler's management and organized labor. Iacocca set the example by cutting his own salary to $1 per year, but the leadership of Douglas Fraser of the UAW was also important.

The infusion of new money allowed Chrysler to develop the K-car line of efficient, front-wheel-drive vehicles. A quality product, aggressive personal advertising by Iacocca (which he saw the need of, but resisted), and an exceptionally strong warranty greatly boosted Chrysler's sales and profits. By 1983 the company was making more money than at any time in its history and was able to pay back all it owed to the government seven years early. Victory had come; but it had been close, and at a cost to many at Chrysler.

Straight Talk (46 pages, 4 chapters)

Iacocca believes that the mandatory use of seat belts would be the one best approach to making driving safer. He also thinks air bags are a bad idea.

Iacocca supports high wages for auto workers, in part because they deserve it and in part because a large middle class is the backbone of American prosperity. Labor costs have gotten out of hand because in fat times auto executives have given in to demands for unlimited cost of living allowances, retirement after 30 years on the job, and extensive medical benefits.

Japan has prospered because it looks out for its own self-interests. Iacocca believes America should do the same. That means replacing free trade with "fair trade" by protecting industries that face protected competition from abroad and by equalizing currency exchange rates.

Finally, America can get its budget deficits under control by cutting spending from both domestic and military programs and raising taxes on imported oil. We also need a coherent national industrial policy that would look to the future by encouraging R&D and the training of more engineers and scientists. We must also end unproductive mergers and lower interest rates so that there will be more money directed toward creating jobs and prosperity.

Epilogue (3 pages)

Iacocca took on the chairmanship of the committee restoring the Statue of Liberty as a tribute to the memory of his immigrant parents and as a statement of belief in American values.

❁❁❁

The book has no references or suggestions for further reading. There is an index.

Evaluation

Presentation

Lee Iacocca the executive has a strong personal style. **Iacocca** the book is a good match for him—which says a lot both for Iacocca as an author and for his collaborator, William Novak, a professional writer. We came up with a raft of adjectives to define the character of the book; according to your feelings about Iacocca, select several of the following:

—outspoken, straight-shooting, blunt, honest, tough;
—opinionated, authoritative, self-serving;
—personal, sentimental, inspiring, provocative;
—preachy, pretentious, moralistic;
—incisive, earthy, profane....

You get the idea by now, we're sure, that the book is not bland or dull. Nor is it deeply illuminating or profound. **Iacocca** does not pause for reflection. It rushes through short punchy chapters, quick-stepping from topic to topic in very short, declarative sentences that barely cling together to form paragraphs.

Iacocca does have some good stories, mostly pretty short. Occasionally one surprises you by being quite funny. The prose yields to cliché far too often, but the author's meaning is always perfectly clear. Moral lessons are introduced at key junctures of the narrative; they tend to have all the sophistication of popular magazines of an earlier era (*The Saturday Evening Post,* for instance), which doesn't mean they lack validity. Management lessons crop up more often. They are not particularly complicated either, but they are pertinent. We may, after all, find it easier to disregard Mr. Iacocca's political and moral philosophies than we can his opinions on how to run a company.

Content

It is difficult to decide just how much of substance we can take away from **Iacocca.** That is, how much is generalizable from his story in either the personal or business realms? We're going to yield to temptation at this juncture and leave that judgment to the individual reader.

We would only like to remake the point, however, that there is an intermittant (essentially unorganized), attempt throughout the text to go beyond "setting the record straight." The *organized* attempt at lesson drawing comes in the final "straight talk" chapters. These are presumably designed to focus public awareness on some key issues of concern to the auto industry while Mr. Iacocca has an interested and respectful audience. The author's opinions are well-articulated, if simply argued (much like a political speech), and worth a close look.

Yet, for all our speculation on the reasons for and importance of autobiographies here and in the Audience and Intentions section, the value of **Iacocca** turns out to be its insider's account of the doings at Ford and Chrysler. Truth be told, we don't become particularly interested in Lee Iacocca as a person, but we do become immersed in his struggles in the auto industry. As mentioned earlier, we may not swallow whole the motivations he ascribes for himself, but we come to trust his recordings of events in Detroit, Washington, and New York.

The book is, in short, fascinating. Without any attempt at sensationalism, it can grip your interest the way prime time television soap operas do for many who enjoy big business fantasies. **Iacocca** has it all: the rise and fall of fortunes, eccentric millionaires, passion, power plays, celebrities, greed, warmth, and so on. There are even commercials.

If you like Iacocca the executive, buy the book. If you want to get an inside view of top management at Ford and the Chrysler turnaround, even if you find Iacocca annoying, you can still buy the book.

Reading Suggestions

If you're more interested in the auto industry or just the turmoil of the past few years than in Lee Iacocca, you might want to skim or skip the first few chapters. If you mainly want the story and are not aroused by Iacocca's views on auto safety or industrial policy, you could skip the concluding "straight talk" section.

That last section is the only one that makes any distinctive break in the text. Some of the chapters jump around in time a little, especially those with points to make about good management. Even if you're only concerned with the Chrysler turnaround, give them all a try. The chapters are short, and the pace is very quick.

Our favorite chapters are 1 (his father), 4 (McNamara and the bean counters), 5 (management), 13 (Chrysler's history), 15 (team building), 20 (equality of sacrifices), and 21 (getting the banks to go along). Car buffs will enjoy chapters 6 and 7 on the Mustang and the Mercury.

Ordering Information:	Available in bookstores everywhere
Specify:	ISBN 0-553-05067-2
Price:	$17.95

Intrapreneuring: Why You Don't Have to Leave the Corporation to Become an Entrepreneur

Gifford Pinchot III

Harper & Row

© 1985
368 pages

Evaluation: This very professionally presented book provides an excellent mixture of conceptual thinking and practical applications. It promotes the idea of "intrapreneuring" (entrepreneuring within the corporation) and also explains both how to be an "intrapreneur" and how to create a corporate environment conducive to "intrapreneuring."

Thesis: Corporations must innovate to survive; the best method is to encourage creative people to become entrepreneurs within the company structure ("intrapreneurs") by allowing them to earn the freedom and resources ("intracapital") with which to pursue their visions (establish "intraprises").

Audience: Managers who have the potential and desire to become "intrapreneurs"; CEOs who want to facilitate innovation.

Reading Time: 8 to 10 hours.

Author

Gifford Pinchot III is a consultant on intrapreneuring and the founder of the School for Intrapreneurs at the Tarrytown Conference Center in New York. He is a man with diverse experiences and educational background and is also an inventor.

Audience and Intentions

Pinchot contends that innovation is stagnating in large organizations as a result of entrenched analysis and control systems—just at the time when new competition is making innovation necessary for survival. The problem is compounded by venture capitalists bidding away the most creative people in the organization and thus freeing them to become *entre*preneurs.

The solution, Pinchot believes, is *intra*preneuring—entrepreneuring within the corporation—a system for speeding up innovation inside an organization. "Intrapreneurs," he explains, "introduce and produce new products, processes, and services, which in turn enable the company as a whole to grow and profit."

Contrary to common opinion, neither entrepreneurs nor intrapreneurs are motivated by money. Instead, they are driven by a personal need to achieve. Corporations can thus retain their innovative people and reap the benefits of their innovations by providing the freedom and resources intrapreneurs require to pursue their goals. Firms must learn how to manage the process of intrapreneuring and establish a system by which intrapreneurs can earn funds to back their projects—what Pinchot calls "intracapital."

The purpose of the book is to explain how "corporations and intrapreneurs interact" so that (1) those who want the freedom to innovate can succeed within the system and (2) CEOs can "create an environment supportive of innovation and intrapreneuring." In more general terms, Pinchot also wants to help begin the process of honoring and empowering intrapreneurs by recognizing their importance the way we do entrepreneurs, inventors, and top executives.

Intrapreneuring is written primarily for two audiences: potential intrapreneurs and their CEOs. It is not a book about beating the system; it is, rather, a guide to shaping the system for innovative use: an enterprise (or "intraprise") made easier by the efforts of all.

Summary

Part I: The Intrapreneurs

Chapter 1: The New Intrapreneurial Spirit (29 pages)

The entrepreneurial spirit can be an important competitive advantage, especially if harnessed in large organizations, which contain some of our best people and resources. But to accomplish this, large corporations must grant employees the kinds of freedoms entrepreneurs now enjoy. In the right environment, freedom and cooperation will generate productivity.

Innovation involves turning new ideas (inventions) into business successes. Large corporations are good at creating ideas but poor at developing them commercially. Dissatisfied would-be intrapreneurs are then driven to venture capitalists to become entrepreneurs. To keep their creative people and implement new ideas, firms must first understand the complicated process by which innovation really works.

Both top management and potential innovators must also recognize certain truths about intrapreneurs. They circumvent or ignore orders, follow intuition, go beyond formal job descriptions, share responsibility with a team, and pursue goals passionately but realistically.

Chapter 2: Who Is the Intrapreneur? (33 pages)

Intrapreneurs bridge the gap between inventors and managers; they take new ideas and turn them into profitable realities. Without them there is an innovation gap. They have vision and the courage to realize it. They can imagine what business and organizational realities will follow from the way customers respond to their innovations; they can plot the necessary steps from idea to actualization.

To make things work, intrapreneurs cross organizational boundaries to do other people's jobs. They have a need to act, and they don't wait for permission to begin. Their dedication frequently shuts out other concerns, including family life. They pursue only goals that they set, that have personal meaning. Successful intrapreneurs learn to overcome mistakes and to manage risk. The typical intrapreneurial personality lies somewhere between that of the traditional manager and that of the traditional entrepreneur.

Chapter 3: Making the Argument for Intrapreneuring (20 pages)

Intrapreneurs are enough like entrepreneurs to make top management nervous, because of the unsettling myths about the entrepreneurial personality. Contrary to prevailing opinion, (1) entrepreneurs are driven by a need to realize their vision, not a desire for wealth; (2) they work to *minimize* risk in order to realize their goals; (3) they follow both intuition and hard analysis; (4) they are honest with themselves and others; and (5) they do not have a need for power. They are, in short, worthy of freedom and responsibility.

Part II: Becoming an Intrapreneur

Chapter 4: Why Intrapreneuring Can Be Better than Entrepreneuring (14 pages)

Big companies can make the development of a new idea far easier for an intrapreneur than the same task would be for an entrepreneur. They offer marketing clout, a technology base, trusted co-workers, and information resources. They can provide financial support for projects that would not be attractive to venture capitalists. On the other hand, entrepreneurs escape the indecisiveness of the corporation, tap the experience of sophisticated venture capitalists, and enjoy the satisfactions of ownership.

Chapter 5: Choosing an Idea (25 pages)

Successful intrapreneurs must choose the right idea from several they might be developing simultaneously in their minds. The idea must be good for the market, good for the company, and good for the intrapreneur. The idea will fit the market if there is a real customer need and the product can be delivered in a cost effective manner at a price that gives adequate margins. It should also be appropriate for the company culture and lead to growth and profits. Most important, the idea should fit the intrapreneur's skills and experience. It should inspire belief, enjoyment, and dedication.

Ideas can come from brainstorming, talking with co-workers in diverse departments, individual curiosity, market research, and current company projects and technology. Intrapreneuring can also involve improving a process within the corporation.

Chapter 6: Planning Your Intraprise (17 pages)

Business planning converts intuitive vision into an action agenda. It documents destination, strategies, schedule, expected obstacles, and expected responses. The planning process includes training yourself to become more entrepreneurial, screening your ideas, attracting a venture team, building team consensus, raising money, and getting permission to proceed. Be careful to whom you show your business plan. Before it is formally presented, you should presell the idea to the decision makers. In writing the plan, begin with your goals and then follow a table of events.

Chapter 7: Identifying Sponsors, the Protectors of New Ideas (31 pages)

Sponsors break down three barriers to intrapreneuring: lack of resources, "nervous money" (that is, vacillating investors), and political attacks. Sponsors are involved with technical problems, marketing options, presentation of ideas to management, and behind-the-scenes intervention. They help the intrapreneur think through and execute the "Intraprise." Sponsors can be CEOs, former intrapreneurs, and owners. They must, however, be attracted naturally when the chemistry is right, not recruited. Above all, there must be trust between intrapreneur and sponsor.

Chapter 8: The Intrapreneurial Way of Leadership (19 pages)

Intrapreneurial leaders face a basic paradox: the new venture team needs decisive centralized direction-setting but, at the same time, it requires participatory management to do its best work.

Successful leaders breed a hybrid organization. They set the direction, give team members freedom and respect, and listen to colleagues—but they make the final decision. They build commitment by focusing on the goal of the intraprise and by sharing the visionary task.

Building an intraprise includes four phases. The first is the solo phase in which the intrapreneur works alone. The second is the network phase in which ideas are shared with a few close friends and trusted customers. This evolves into the bootleg phase where the emerging team works unofficially during spare hours. Finally, there is the formal team phase, which requires delicate management of people and the mainline corporate structure.

Part III: Building the Intrapreneurial Environment

Chapter 9: The Freedom Factors: Can Intrapreneuring Happen in Your Company? (65 pages)

The presence or absence of 10 freedom factors determines how effective intrapreneurs can be in their corporate culture. Potential innovators and managers seeking to promote innovation should audit their company's environment for the following:

1. Self-selection: Does the company encourage the self-appointed intrapreneur?
2. No handoffs: Does the company provide ways for intrapreneurs to stay with their intraprises?
3. The doer decides: Can people do the job in their own way without always seeking permission?
4. Corporate slack: Are there quick and informal ways to gain access to resources for new ideas?
5. Ending the home-run philosophy: Can the company manage many small and experimental products and businesses?
6. Tolerance of risk, failure, and mistakes: Is risk-taking encouraged? Are people allowed to learn from mistakes?
7. Patient money: Can the company stick with the experiment through several false starts?
8. Freedom from turfiness: Are people more concerned with new ideas or defending their turf?

9. Cross-functional teams: Is it easy to form autonomous teams?

10. Multiple options: Are people free to use the resources of other divisions and outside vendors?

Chapter 10: Rewards along the Intrapreneurial Career Path (16 pages)

The reward systems for most firms are inadequate because they (1) don't match the risks of intrapreneuring; (2) feature promotions, which are not suitable for most intrapreneurs; and (3) ignore the freedom to act on new projects, which is the basic motivation of the intrapreneur. Reward systems discourage risk-taking and encourage failure avoidance. They must be restructured to acknowledge the extraordinary contributions of the innovators. Firms should create a career path for intrapreneurs that allows the continual inception of new ventures without the financial penalties of lost promotions and with the increased freedom to act.

Chapter 11: Intracapital: Freedom as a Reward (24 pages)

The most fundamental measure of progress for an intrapreneur is the increasing freedom to use corporate resources to build new businesses for the corporation. This reward can be given (earned, actually) in the form of "intracapital."

Intracapital is a permanent discretionary budget; like a bank account, it is there until used. It is a powerful motivator because it conveys a sense of ownership and guarantees freedom. It is advantageous to the company because it encourages frugality and allows the firm to bet on proven winners.

Intrapreneurs earn intracapital when their new ventures succeed for the corporation. In a formal system, intrapreneurs also take some risks, such as foregone salary increases and extra, unpaid labor; there is an agreed-upon method of measuring success; profits are allocated to sponsors and team members, as well, in an agreed-upon manner; and earned rewards and autonomy can not be taken away.

Chapter 12: Putting to Rest the Fears of Anarchy (13 pages)

Contrary to many people's initial fears, intrapreneurial corporations are better controlled than hierarchical organizations. The essence of efficient control is a good fit between the system and the task. Intrapreneurial firms are fit for the Innovation Age because they conserve the resource of brain power. Such firms have found that trusting their people to preserve high quality works. In fact, with the increased use of computers, smaller staffs will be possible, thus lessening the chances of overcontrol. In the Innovation Age, control systems will be based on selecting and empowering the right people, much as the venture capital system functions today.

Conclusion: The Renaissance Corporation (10 pages)

To survive, corporations of the future must change. They must balance necessary structures and freedom of action to increase productivity. The first step is an "interactive decentralization" that relies on voluntary customer-vendor relationships. Executives can create an internal marketplace that pushes intrapreneurs and employees toward the objectives of the corporation. Intracapital is the key ingredient in making decentralization work because it generates free *intra*prise. Intrapreneurship is a way of organizing business so that work again becomes joyful. The wealth of corporations—like that of nations—is dependent on the freedom of their people.

Appendix: Intraprise Plan Guidelines (29 pages)

The author analyzes nine elements of a business plan as they would apply to an intrapreneurial venture. He offers advice and raises questions that an intrapreneur must answer before proceeding.

* * *

Quotations and statistics are documented throughout the chapters in footnotes. The author also provides a bibliography for further reading and an index.

Evaluation

Presentation

Pinchot has produced a very fine piece of professional literature. The book is clearly written, evenly paced, and carefully (and well) argued. There is a nice level-headed calmness to *Intrapreneuring*—a quality missing from many other serious treatments of important business subjects. The author's chief professional concern is the promotion of intrapreneurship. His personal experiences (the "I" that seems to be everywhere in management books) intrude very seldom. Here, the idea has precedence over the ego.

Intrapreneuring offers an excellent balance of abstract concept and practical example, of reason and experience. In addition, seven of the chapters conclude with extended profiles of intrapreneurs. These well-focused case studies do a good job of getting Pinchot's main points across. The only drawback is that the examples seem limited to a relatively few firms. We seem to meet the people at 3M in every chapter. But this is probably a natural result of Pinchot's stress on depth over breadth.

In *Intrapreneuring*, lots of little things are done right: the layout makes for easy reading; the figures are clear and significantly enhance the text; the documentation is good, and so on. We understand better after reading a well-crafted book how people like Tom Peters (*A Passion for Excellence*) can get so excited about what seem to be small matters of business. In books as well as management, the little things do make a difference.

Content

Just as the presentation contains a good mixture of the abstract and concrete, so too does the material presented. *Intrapreneuring* is a book of ideas and applications, of theory and practice. Pinchot is, first of all, selling the concept of intrapreneurship and its importance. He asserts that (1) innovation in corporations is necessary for their survival; (2) the push for entrepreneurial freedom is strong and will if necessary be satisfied outside the corporation by venture capitalism (and by foreign firms); and (3) entrepreneurial innovation can be harnessed, indeed encouraged, within the corporation through the intrapreneuring process.

The possibility for and necessity of innovation within large organizations is supported in the latest work of Peter Drucker:*

> Today's businesses, especially the large ones, simply will not survive in this period of rapid change and innovation unless they acquire entrepreneurial competence.... It is the existing business—and the fair-sized rather than the small one—that has the best capability for entrepreneurial leadership. (p. 144)

Pinchot does not cite Drucker's newest book, nor does Drucker mention "intrapreneuring," but the two authors were clearly writing to much the same purpose.

Pinchot restricts his theoretical discussions to the first three chapters and to the opening and closing comments directed at CEOs. His primary goals are (1) to explain to interested managers how to become an intrapreneur (chapters 4–8 and the appendix) and (2) to explain to top management how to structure a corporate environment conducive to intrapreneuring (chapters 9–12). These chapters are dedicated to convincing both potential intrapreneur and CEO that the process is possible. They are effective because they are detailed, analytical, and honest.

Pinchot has had more than a little experience presenting the idea of intrapreneuring, and he has well-considered responses to everyone's concerns. We are not left with the feeling of having discovered an easy solution to encouraging and managing innovation, but we do have a sense of possessing comprehensive guidelines that could work.

Pinchot believes that the wealth of corporations will increase as corporations give freedom to their employees, that is, as they empower intrapreneurs. His book gives corporate managers the insight and instruction to begin that process.

**Innovation and Entrepreneurship* (Harper & Row, 1985). *Reviewed in 3, no. 3 of BBR;* reprinted in this volume.

Reading Suggestions

Make sure you take a look at all the material outside the chapters themselves: read the preface, the appendix, and the opening and closing memos to the CEOs. Also be sure not to skip the profiles of intrapreneurs at the end of chapters 1–4, 6, 7, and 9; they are excellent. The natural breaks in reading come at the major divisions (after chapters 3, 8, and 12), but only chapters 10 and 11 are close companions.

This is one of those fine books that frequently make you stop to reflect on how the author's message can be applied to your organization. Those are the valuable moments to take notes and enjoy some hard thinking.

Ordering Information: Harper & Row
10 East 53rd Street
New York, New York 10022

Call: (212) 207-7000

Specify: ISBN 0-06-015305-9

Price: $19.95

Quality Without Tears: The Art of Hassle-Free Management

Philip B. Crosby

McGraw-Hill

© 1984
205 pages

Evaluation: An efficiently written book that presents a concept of quality in very concrete terms and defines the scope of a comprehensive education and implementation process.

Thesis: Quality is achievable through management commitment to cultural change; consistent attention to, and insistence on, high standards; organization-wide training in quality; and creation of a hassle-free, nonbureaucratic work environment.

Audience: Top management in both service and manufacturing industries; any manager with the drive for quality improvement and the initiative to instigate change.

Reading Time: 4 to 5 hours.

Author

Philip B. Crosby is the chairman of Philip Crosby Associates, a management consulting firm, and a teacher at The Quality College, an institution he founded in 1979. He was corporate vice president at ITT for 14 years and is the author of *Quality Is Free* (1979).

Audience and Intentions

It appears that **Quality Without Tears** is part of a professional quest that began with the success of Crosby's first book and the author's subsequent departure from ITT to found his own quality-consulting firm. As Crosby explains in his preface:

> The urge to get out in the world and see whether I could get American management to see the light was just too strong. Quality was fast becoming a lost item because management was so incredibly naive about it. The "workers" were being blamed for what the management was causing.

Crosby reports that he has witnessed some progress in the few years that followed—and that he and his colleagues have learned much about consulting and guiding people toward quality. That process, he says, always begins with "understanding."

The purpose of the book then is "to help the reader understand more about quality improvement and the concepts that make it happen." And Crosby makes it plain that he has not written a "cookbook"—that is, a series of recipes for easy success. He intends his work to further "comprehension and communication" as the beginning of the "cultural revolution that is required."

Crosby contends that gearing an organization toward the consistent attainment of a high quality standard necessitates basic adjustments in its corporate culture. He believes that quality improvement is the same as hassle elimination. It is not possible, he contends, to create quality with bureaucratic controls; rather, it must be attained through a comprehensive (and ongoing) process involving determination, education, and implementation.

Crosby's approach treats the whole corporation or independent division. The ultimate audience for his book is, by inference, high level managers with sufficient authority to initiate the process.

Quality Without Tears can, however, prove useful for any manager with the need to work in a quality-oriented organization and the drive to achieve that ambition.

Summary

Chapter 1: The Profile of a Problem Organization (5 pages)

When people are dissatisfied with the final product or service there is trouble with quality. Organizations in trouble show five symptoms. (1) The product/service contains deviations from the agreed-upon requirements. (2) An extensive field service or dealer network is needed to keep the customers happy. (3) Management does not provide a clear performance standard or definition of quality. (4) Management does not know the price of nonconformance to standards. (5) Management denies that it is the cause of the problem. This last item is the most critical because the main obstacle to improvement is the stubbornness of management.

Chapter 2: The Quality Vaccine (8 pages)

Quality troubles usually result from short-term solutions to schedule or cost problems. The vaccine for the resulting nonconformance does *not* involve detailed procedures and controls. Instead, antibodies that prevent hassle must be built into the management style of decision making. To prepare the vaccine and continually administer it requires a strategy consisting of three distinct managerial actions: (1) determination to achieve quality, (2) education of all managers and employees about their individual roles in the improvement process, and (3) implementation on a continuous basis. This last step entails changing the corporate culture to forever dehassle the organization.

Chapter 3: Demotivation (22 pages)

Motivational speakers and products are part of a growth industry that shouldn't even exist. Our employees shouldn't need to be "turned on" because they were already motivated when they started with the company. They are *de*motivated by the normal, thoughtless, irritating, unconcerned operating practices of the organization.

Hassled employees feel like adults who are being treated like children. Hassled people do not produce quality work; they spend more time working on each other than they do making the firm's product or service. In a hassle-prone company, management and employees are on different sides.

The process of running a hassle-free company involves many actions and policies. But everything that is done must be realistic, consistent, and imaginative. Dehassling a business is a process, not a program. You never complete a process.

Chapter 4: A Quality Carol (17 pages)

Tightfisted Emory Spellman meets the ghost of his former partner, Jacob Masters, who tells him "the way to make money is to give the customers what they were promised and eliminate the hassle for the employees." Spellman is visited by the ghosts of quality past, present, and future. They reveal to him the costs of nonconformance to standards, the role of management in shaping a quality-oriented corporate culture, and the threat to the business if management fails to act.

The lessons of the ghosts are that, despite conventional wisdom, (1) quality is conformance to requirements, (2) prevention is the only system that works, (3) specific standards such as zero defects must be applied, and (4) the price of nonconformance should be calculated. Spellman sees the light and vows to create a hassle-free company.

Chapter 5: Determination (6 pages)

Companies must be determined if they wish to improve. But even determined companies will fail to improve when (1) the effort is called a program (with a conclusion) rather than a process (endless), (2) all effort is aimed at the lower levels, (3) the quality control people are cynical, and (4) management is impatient for results.

Nothing happens until management decides to clean up its own act: that is, to take product and service requirements seriously. Management must continually show that it is in it for the long haul, forever, to maintain credibility.

Chapter 6: The First Absolute: The Definition of Quality Is Conformance to Requirements (7 pages)

Quality improvement is getting everyone to *d*o *i*t *r*ight the *f*irst *t*ime (DIRFT). Management must (1) establish the requirements that the employees are to meet, (2) supply what the employees need to meet those requirements, and (3) spend all its time encouraging and helping them. Hassle comes about because of vacillation in management's dedication. The determined executive must define quality precisely as a conformance to requirements and never allow any deviations.

Chapter 7: The Second Absolute: The System of Quality Is Prevention (8 pages)

Manufacturing and service companies are often preoccupied with appraisal: inspecting and testing after the fact. Appraisal is an expensive and unreliable way of getting quality. A better system is prevention, because the error that does not exist cannot be missed. The secret of prevention is to identify opportunities for error and then take steps to control them. One such technique is statistical quality control. SQC is difficult but possible; managers are reluctant to undertake it, unfortunately, because it involves interrupting the normal flow.

Chapter 8: The Third Absolute: The Performance Standard Is Zero Defects (11 pages)

A company is an organism with millions of actions that must be done just as planned for the products/services to come out right. The performance standard is a device for helping individuals to realize the importance of each little action. Unfortunately, companies adopt requirements of "shipped-product quality level" and "acceptable quality level" that establish an expectation of error and thus convince people that the determination to get things done right is lacking.

In contrast, the Zero Defects standard thwarts the self-fulfilling prophecy of error by requiring that jobs be done right the first time. Most U.S. firms have chosen to consider ZD as a motivation program; ITT and the Japanese have adopted it completely, with very good results.

Chapter 9: The Fourth Absolute: The Measurement of Quality Is the Price of Nonconformance (2 pages)

The price of nonconformance is the expense involved in doing things wrong—the costs of corrections and warranties. These add up to 20 percent or more of sales in manufacturing companies and 35 percent of operating costs in service companies. In contrast, the price of conformance—what is necessary to spend to make things come out right—includes the cost of prevention and education and represents 3 to 4 percent of sales in a well-run company.

Chapter 10: Education (10 pages)

Making a cookbook for something like hassle elimination only adds to the problem because it creates an additional set of procedures. Producing a hassle-free company requires the continual transfer of information from person to person. Education must become routine.

A systematic plan includes executive education, in which senior management learns its role; management education, in which the middle levels learn how to implement the process; employee education, in which all workers learn their responsibilities; and workshops, in which functional departments such as marketing learn how they fit into the quality process. Throughout, education teaches the six C's: comprehension, commitment, competence, communication, correction, and continuance.

Chapter 11: Implementation (9 pages)

Implementation means changing the culture and management style of the company. It must be approached in a methodical manner as a matter of corporate priority. It is a continuous process of changing values and attitudes.

Since the problem today is getting employees to believe that the company really means what it says, the first step in the 14-step process of implementation is management commitment. That involves three actions: (1) issuing a corporate policy statement on quality, (2) making quality the first item of all management status meetings, and (3) having the CEO and COO constantly delivering quality speeches as they go around the company. Management commitment will be tested until it can be assumed.

Chapter 12: Team Actions (8 pages)

The second step is to put together a quality improvement team to guide the process by coordinating and supporting actions. The team should represent all operational functions; the chair should have access to top management.

The third step in implementing quality is to establish realistic measurement standards. Hassle doesn't come from measurement; it comes from unclear standards.

Step 4 consists of setting up a procedure, involving the comptroller and other interested parties, to calculate the cost of quality.

In step 5, the workforce is made aware of the emphasis on quality by any means possible for spreading information.

Step 6 sets up a corrective action system with the goals of identifying and eliminating problems forever by determining root causes.

Chapter 13: Team Executions (11 pages)

Step 7 in the process of implementation is Zero Defects planning: making ready for Zero Defects Day, which comes about 18 months into the process.

Step 8 occurs when management finally understands the four Absolutes of Quality Management and can begin educating all the employees by means of a complete system that can provide a standard message.

Zero Defects Day allows management to make a public commitment to quality. This celebration is step 9.

While Zero Defects is the ultimate goal, setting up intermediate goals is step 10.

Step 11 is error-cause removal. It involves asking people to state the problems they have so that something can be done about them.

Step 12 is recognition. Each company devises a specific way to recognize hard-working employees. This provides a clear description of quality performance and examples to emulate.

Quality councils, step 13, bring quality professionals together to let them learn from each other.

Finally, step 14 repeats the whole process by turning responsibilities over to a new quality improvement team after the original group has served for approximately two years.

Chapter 14: The Saving of Emory Spellman (17 pages)

The hero of the Dickensian tale told in chapter 4 returns to evaluate his company according to the criteria established in chapter 1. He and his management team discover they have all the symptoms of a seriously ailing firm.

Spellman and associates decide to create a hassle-free company. Their first action is to help the comptroller calculate the price of nonconformance. They next bring all the thought leaders of the company together, divide into groups, identify the ten biggest problems of quality in the company, and make suggestions for action.

Spellman creates a quality improvement team to coordinate the firm's efforts. Executives go off to quality management sessions and set up an in-house education system for all employees.

After the first year of the process great improvement has been made. Zero Defects Day is held, and a new team takes over coordination responsibilities. Spellman continues to press for quality, however, recognizing that the process never stops.

Chapter 15: The Dehassling of Lightblue (6 pages)

A company famous for its elaborate planning system discovers that it has been in love with planning for its own sake. Management decides to dehassle the process, making planning a servant of the company rather than the other way around.

Chapter 16: Some Success Stories (7 pages)

The many successes in quality improvement that the author has seen over the years have several characteristics in common. All companies report (1) better communications, (2) lowered costs of quality, (3) fewer errors in paperwork, (4) a reduction in data entry errors, (5) less need for skilled field service, (6) a lowering of the hassle level, and (7) better administration.

Chapter 17: Mixing the Vaccination Serum (17 pages)

Setting up a permanent system to eliminate hassle and institute quality improvement requires careful attention to the five basic ingredients: integrity, systems, communications, operations, and policies.

The CEO, COO, senior executives, managers, professional employees, and regular workers must all be committed to the integrity of requirements of quality products/services. Systems must be established for the management function, education, financial measurement, customer satisfaction, and defect prevention. A communications system focuses on disseminating information about progress, recognizing employee achievement, and identifying nonconformance to standards. An operations system concentrates on educating suppliers on the company's quality needs and constantly examining procedures for possible improvement. Policies clearly emphasize quality for all aspects of the business.

Chapter 18: How Come Very Little Ever Improves All by Itself? (3 pages)

American business has had all its problems with quality because it doesn't take the subject seriously. It must become as concerned about quality as it is about profit. When management respects the rights of customers exactly the way it respects the rights of banks and stockholders, then quality will happen all the time. When freeing the employees of hassles is considered as important as increasing sales, then hassles will be eliminated.

Guidelines for Browsers (26 pages)

This section repeats the key statements of the book, in an easy-to-read list format, in the order in which they appear in the chapters. Page numbers are provided.

* * *

Quality Without Tears contains no footnotes or references. Nor does the author provide a bibliography for further study. The index is appropriate for the size and character of the book.

Evaluation

Presentation

Quality Without Tears is written with absolutely no wasted motion—which is too bad. Crosby's book is very well organized and efficient, to the point of being too abrupt and too sparse. In the early chapters in particular, important charts and tables are left unexplained.

That is not to say, however, that **Quality** is not clear about its main points or without charm. Crosby delivers his message about quality and hassle precisely and emphatically. He uses a great many metaphors, some to good effect. There are several clever passages, not excepting his variation of *A Christmas Carol* in chapter 4.

Crosby handles examples very well. They are succinct and right on the money. The author has chosen not to name specific companies or CEOs in his case histories, except for the one or two references to ITT (Crosby's old firm). Without such formal documentation we must rely completely on the integrity of the author for their accuracy but there is no reason to question this.

On the whole, we respect the intensity of Crosby's convictions. We have a sense that he urgently wants us (and everyone) to take to heart this concept of quality, but he refrains from preaching or shouting. The book retains its professionalism; it is personal but not familiar.

Content

Throughout **Quality**, Crosby sticks to his promise to stress comprehension of basic concepts and not produce a "cookbook" for quality improvement. Thus he provides the reader with a core of ideas. Briefly, these are:

1. Quality is an ongoing, never-ending process, not a transitory motivational program.
2. Quality is only possible in a nonbureaucratic environment that does not hassle employees.
3. Quality means: (a) conformance to requirements (standards), (b) prevention rather than appraisal, (c) meeting a performance standard of zero defects, and (d) calculating costs in terms of nonconformance (expense of doing things wrong).
4. All managers and employees must be educated in the language and process of quality.
5. Implementation means changing the corporate culture and decision-making style of management.

Crosby believes strongly that quality is a way of life, not a technique of management. It should mean as much to the company as profits. He believes in changing the corporate lifestyle *forever*, not briefly tinkering.

In the end, Crosby succeeds in convincing us that quality is good business and can be achieved, although at times he seems a little too sure that his own prescription for success is the only one worth following. He sold his approach to the Japanese in 1964 with results they appreciate many years later (they gave him a party in 1980). He hopes that this book—supported by his companies—will inspire U.S. managers with the possibilities of quality improvement. It is a message we might all do well to examine seriously.

Reading Suggestions

Some of the tabular material in chapters 1 and 2 is not developed until chapters 14 and 17; so a little patience is required early. Chapters 5–9 are companions, as are chapters 11–13, and each is best read as a set. A little selective skimming over the "Spellman" and "Lightblue" stories (part of chapter 3, all of chapters 4, 14, and 15) might be in order. The rest of the first half of the book deserves close attention. The unusual "Guidelines for Browsers" is probably best used for review or later reference.

Ordering Information:	McGraw-Hill Book Company 1221 Avenue of the Americas New York, New York 10020
Call:	(212) 512-2000
Specify:	ISBN 0-07-014530-X
Price:	$18.95

The 100 Best Companies to Work for in America

Robert Levering, Milton Moskowitz, and Michael Katz

Addison-Wesley

© 1984
372 pages

Evaluation: A clever, perceptive, and engaging set of profiles of a wide range of companies. Each short chapter rates the company for pay, benefits, job security, chance to move up, and ambience while defining its special character. The introduction and epilog draw some conclusions about the criteria for a "good" company from the employee point of view. Lists at the back of the book arrange companies by industry and location.

Thesis: There are good companies to work for throughout a broad range of industries and in locations all over the country. The best work places break down the authoritarian barriers between management and employees.

Audience: For managers who want to improve the quality of work life at their company and for those looking for greener pastures elsewhere.

Reading Time: 5 to 10 minutes per profile; 10 to 12 hours for the whole book.

Authors

Robert Levering, Milton Moskowitz, and Michael Katz constitute a team of experienced business journalists and researchers. They are the authors of *Everybody's Business: An Almanac* (Harper & Row, 1980), which profiled over 300 large companies.

Audience and Intentions

Journalists have their own set of pretensions. The authors (journalists all) make no statements of purpose or grandiose claims for their work, other than faithfulness to professional technique. A journalistic perspective proclaims: here's something enlightening and interesting, for anyone who wants to read it, to put to whatever use in whatever way they wish. "Just the facts, ma'am, just the facts"—although we'll try to be as clever as we can when presenting them.

Publishers, however, have a different agenda. The publicity people at Addison-Wesley are willing to define several objectives the book might fulfill. Happily, we are able to agree with them and even add some of our own perceptions. We believe, in short, that **The 100 Best Companies to Work for in America** performs four functions. It will:

1. Help job hunters find a "good" place to work.
2. Provide job hunters with a set of criteria by which to evaluate prospective employers in addition to the 100 companies profiled.
3. Supply managers with information on the corporate style and employee relations of successful firms.
4. Identify for managers what constitutes a "good company to work for" so that those qualities might be instilled in their own organizations.

100 Best is therefore not just a handbook for people seeking other employment, it is also a guide for employers who want their businesses to be better places in which to work. The motivation for the latter should go beyond pride and encompass economic self-interest because, as reported again and again in the book, managers of profiled companies identify dedicated employees as the key to their business success.

The evolution of this book did not, however, begin with the company's point of view (i.e., how to be profitable), but with the employee's (i.e., how to find a great place to work). The authors say that their approach was "journalistic rather than scientific." By that they mean they "did not try to impose a preconceived set of standards." Instead, they polled a host of experts and media sources for names of companies with reputations for being good places in which to work. They narrowed an original list of 350 to 135 by querying the candidates directly about themselves and their employee policies. To make the final cuts and to obtain more details and a personal perspective, they spent a year visiting 114 companies in 27 states, observing and interviewing people at all levels.

From their research the authors identify several common elements in "best companies to work for." They back away, however, from offering observations other than the most general, namely, that such companies break down the traditional "we"–"them" barrier between management and workers and create an authentic "us" atmosphere that includes everyone from the CEO on down. Although Levering, Moskowitz, and Katz admit that readers might draw their own conclusions from the study concerning productive employee management practices, they will stick to their original perspective when defining the principal benefit to be gained from establishing the superior employment conditions described by the book: "a working life for thousands of people really worth living and worth looking forward to every working day."

Contents

Almost the entire book consists of short profiles of the 100 "best" companies. Nearly 90 percent of the profiles run three or four pages; none is shorter than two pages or longer than five. The format of the profiles uniformly contains these elements:

- The company logo.
- The company's formal name, common name, product(s) made or service(s) performed, and number of employees.

- A graphic overview of the company's rating on five criteria relative to others in the book.
- The major plus and major minus associated with the company.
- A narrative description of the quality of work life at the company.
- A list of the main employment centers of the company.
- The address and phone number of company headquarters.

The authors rated the companies according to five criteria: pay, benefits, job security, opportunity to advance, and ambience. Pay scales were compared both to other companies in the industry and the other 99 firms profiled in the book. For benefits the authors considered variety and strength of programs. The highest scores for job security went to those companies with a no-layoff policy. Chances to move up were evaluated on the basis of quality training programs and potential for employees to get to the top. Ambience (environment or atmosphere) was defined by a company's unique qualities or special style of doing business.

The profiles themselves are written in the best journalistic style: quickly paced, sharply focused, economical, and heavily laced with quotations from company people and media. They attempt to capture the special flavor of work life at the company without being too analytical, although the data on benefits, particularly, are there. The tone is informal, almost conversational; each piece is lively and entertaining.

Levering and company have the most fun, however, with the major pluses and minuses that introduce the profiles. Several of the minuses are especially clever if taken in the right ironic spirit. The drawback to working at Celestial Seasonings, for instance, is that "you're surrounded by kids." At General Electric they advise that you don't want to be an antinuclear activist, at Hallmark "a cynic would last about one minute," at Intel "they yell at each other a lot," and with Philip Morris "you get a free carton of cigarettes every week" (a minus).

Of course, always trying to be clever leads to excess on occasion: they warn that the "chemistry" at DuPont "may leave you pining for a breath of fresh air" and that working at Olga (fine-quality undergarments for women) is not for everyone because "some may not think making bras an uplifting experience." Mercifully, such transgressions against good taste are rare, although the authors do yield to the temptation of the easy (and thus suspect) metaphor: for Anheuser-Busch, owner of the St. Louis Baseball Cardinals, the plus is that "you can swing for the fences here"; but "if you don't hit a home run, you might be benched permanently."

Levering and colleagues can also be cryptic. Even after reading the entire entry you may not understand Analog's minus: "a linear place in a digital world." Others—like Raychem's "if you get lost here, you have to find your own way around"—become clear by the end of the profile. More frequently, the pluses and minuses sum up the company in a perceptive and penetrating fashion. They evaluate Hewlett-Packard with: "you get a chance to work with a lot of brainy people who are not stuck on themselves," but "you may be handicapped here if you don't have a degree in electrical engineering—or if you're female." For Johnson & Johnson the analysis is shorter: "they know right from wrong," but the company "tends to be stuffy."

Representative Selections

The authors are not beyond being clever in the text of the profiles either, but they do so in service to a carefully crafted rendering of the essence of the company's work style. Unfortunately, we cannot summarize all 100 profiles. We can, however, demonstrate the character of the book with these samples. While the selections are not random, they are representative, for **100 Best** is of remarkably consistent quality and written in a very even style.

Anheuser-Busch Companies, Inc. Workers at A-B have the competitive spirit of crowds at a football game. They feel they're in a tough fight to remain the number 1 brewery, and they have a lot of pride in their "team." The company also instills a sense of history because of its long tradition and because the St. Louis headquarters is an official landmark.

W.L. Gore & Associates, Inc. Gore makes synthetic fibers that have a variety of uses. The Delaware-based firm is very unstructured. By comparison, "most Silicon Valley companies are about as egalitarian as the U.S. Marine Corps." When a Gore facility grows above 200 employees, it is split apart and the company constructs a new plant.

Intel Corporation. People push each other demonically in a very competitive environment. The company is for high achievers who can work well with others and who have a solid enough identity to withstand frequent evaluation. On the other hand, Intel has no dress codes, and it retains and rewards its people even during hard times.

Merle Norman. The company pampers its people with gourmet meals, fancy outings, free evening entertainment, and beautiful surroundings. Most of the employees are women, and they are given ample opportunity to get ahead. Merle Norman is, however, only for those who can adapt to a certain structure and code of behavior.

Tandy Corporation. The phenomenal growth of the retail chain in the last several years has made millionaires of about 60 employees, and not all high-level executives either. Three-quarters of Tandy employees own stock in the company, and they act like proud owners. The feeling is enhanced by an open door policy and a tradition of promoting from within; all Radio Shack sales employees are considered potential sales managers.

Wal-Mart Stores, Inc. This chain operates only in towns with population under 50,000 people. It has a rah-rah spirit that is almost revivalistic. The founder, Sam Walton, does everything he can to involve his people in the company and evoke an intense family feeling. Personal strokes and numerous awards help keep the enthusiasm welling.

Other Features

The authors also find several other ways to list companies that are both interesting and useful. First, they single out the 10 best companies overall and the 5 runners-up. Next they list the 10 best companies by each of the five criteria—pay, benefits, security, upward mobility, ambience. Third, they arrange the companies by industry. The categories are: consumer goods (16), drugs and health care (6), high technology (19), oil and chemicals (17), steel and auto (10), conglomerate (4), office equipment (13), clothing (6), shelter (6), utility (1), media and entertainment (10), retailing (10), banking and finance (9), insurance (5), transportation (5), and restaurants and hotels (4). Obviously, several companies fit in more than one category. Finally, the 100 best companies are distributed by state.

The book also has a short introduction and an even shorter epilog. We have already discussed much of the information in the introduction; it defines the rating criteria and describes the process of selecting the companies to be profiled. The epilog is a little special. It is entitled "Why McDonald's Didn't Make It." The epilog is an unofficial profile with a pointed message. The authors give McDonald's high marks in several areas but decide to exclude the company even though it is highly regarded in managerial circles. The basis for their rejection is that McDonald's seems "to embrace a system geared to exploiting people in the lower ranks." By the authors' criteria—companies "good for people in the lower ranks as well as in management"—McDonald's doesn't measure up.

Evaluation

Presentation

We've already described the character of the writing; it is clever, sharp, efficient, and highly entertaining. The quality is consistently high, failing only when the authors occasionally succumb to the temptation of cheap wit. Every profile is well written, and many contain distinctive passages. Consider, for instance, the analysis of Control Data Corporation (CDC): "CDC doesn't attract the flamboyant Elmer Gantry-type evangelists; it appeals more to the YMCA-type do-gooders, provided they also possess a strong Calvinist interest in making money."

The authors are considerate of their readers. They define terms and describe product functions sparingly but as needed. They supply all the data on a company that is reasonable for a publication of this scope and still concentrate on portraying the flavor of work life there. That flavor mixes in the downside or limiting ingredients as well. These profiles are not unabashed outpourings of praise. Levering et al. are aware that there is frequently "a gap between what a company preaches and what it practices."

100 Best has, of course, no formal documentation: no bibliography, references, or index. The authors' sources are diverse, although they obviously depend quite heavily upon interviews of employees, local media, and company publications. Because of the journalistic style, quotations from individual employees and public documents are given considerable prominence, and we wonder at times if too few people had too much influence on the authors' perceptions. That is, of course, always a problem when an author (or reviewer) is trying to select a representative sample to exhibit the character of the whole.

The book is very easy to use. Although the profiles are (naturally) arranged alphabetically, there are lists of companies by criteria (pay, benefits, security, upward mobility, ambience), industry, and location. These lists are very valuable features if any of those factors—or some combination—is of overriding concern to the reader. They are also quite revealing. The high technology industry has the most representatives, but consumer goods shows strongly, and there are several companies in the smokestack industries. All but four states are home to a good company. California leads the way by a large margin; Texas and New York are second and third, respectively. Southern states have larger representations for their population bases than northern states.

Content

Some mention needs to be made of the currency of the data. The authors' survey was conducted over an extended period, and some company information was gathered in 1981, some in 1982, some in 1983. The dating is less important if the book is used as a source of ideas for good employee management. Job hunters, in any case, should supplement the book with their own up-to-date research. There are other limitations to this volume as a practical job-seekers' guide. First, a few profiles note that the company has more employee applications on file now than they can process—

indeed, the introduction mentions that some companies declined to participate in the survey for this reason. Second, a few profiles are obviously of little relevance to the mobile manager; Linnton Plywood (a co-op of 189 workers) and the Los Angeles Dodgers are examples.

For any reader—seeking another position or not—**100 Best** engenders good feelings. The authors have managed to picture a vast scope of opportunity for job satisfaction in America. The variety of company type, size, style, and location they profile can accommodate a wide range of personalities and needs (which is one reason they explore Linnton Plywood and the Los Angeles Dodgers along with Hewlett-Packard and 3M). In fact, the diversity of the companies that are good places to work is uplifting in itself. And this is true even though, as noted earlier, **100 Best** is in no sense (to use one of the authors' favorite phrases) a "rah rah" publication.

There are other ancillary benefits to be gained from reading **100 Best.** We obtain, for instance, an understanding of the extent of the damage of the recession of 1981–1983. In profile after profile, we have accounts of how companies were forced to severely revise long-standing layoff and benefits policies to respond to the economic crunch. We also pick up little gems of information that tickle the brain. We were interested to learn, for example, that Heinz owns Weight Watchers, why General Electric was getting out of the toaster business, how McCormick decided to add the Tio Sancho line of Mexican food, and that Ryder delivered 40 percent of the cars built by General Motors.

It is evident that **100 Best** achieves the first three goals we defined earlier in the "Audience and Intentions" section. The book (1) identifies and describes a wide range of good places to work, (2) establishes a set of criteria that can be applied elsewhere, and (3) offers insights into the employee management styles of a number of successful firms. The authors also achieve the fourth objective: defining what constitutes a good company to work for. But that merits further discussion.

The key issue is the principle of selection. The defining attribute for Levering, Moskowitz, and Katz is top management's honest respect for employees (including managers) at every level of the organization. What makes a great place to work? The best summation may be in the philosophy of Tenneco: "We pay well, but we do not believe that pay and benefits are the primary motivators. It's more important that people have a feeling of purpose, self-accomplishment, and belonging."

The authors list 12 specific attributes that many of the superior places to work have in addition to good pay and benefits. They include such things as teamwork, open communications, community participation, and pleasant physical surroundings. Levering and colleagues stop short, however, of declaring that these are *necessary* characteristics of a good company or that this is what a company *must* do to succeed. They have an extremely important point to make: the company policy must be authentic. There must be no feeling of division between management and employees—no "we" and "they." Otherwise, adopting these elements is simply manipulative. People will see them as contrivances, and they will fail.

This distinction appears in the introduction, which is entitled "beyond technique." The title emphasizes the message that an egalitarian attitude is more important than the devices used to create a quality work environment. The process succeeds when key individuals "genuinely care about the quality of work experience of everyone in the company." **100 Best** is thus essentially employee oriented. The authors declare that they know what constitutes a good company to work for but not necessarily what makes for a successful company. That is why, they point out, their list of companies diverges from *In Search of Excellence.* Unlike that popular book, **100 Best** does not assert that all companies should behave along prescribed guidelines because (1) while good employee relations should lead to success, there are other managerial paths to that goal (as with McDonald's, for instance) and (2) implementing these attributes of a good place to work is not as easy as simply imitating other companies—it goes, in other words, "beyond technique."

Ultimately, the theme of the book is very simple. It is, in fact, the same as what is taught in a good educational psychology course: "everybody has to be somebody." Everyone, that is, needs to share in the feeling of purpose, self-accomplishment, and belonging described earlier. **100 Best** profiles a number of diverse companies that have successfully applied that lesson. For any of us who do not already work in such a company, they can be either places to run to or places to emulate.

Reading Suggestions

How you use the book will depend on whether you are looking for a haven somewhere else or ways to make your present company into one. If you are looking for a job, you'll probably want to consult the lists in the back of the book to search according to industry, location, or criteria (pay, benefits, etc.). You can, of course, employ the hit or miss method—choosing companies you know or are interested in—or proceed systematically (and alphabetically) from front to back.

It can take from less than 5 minutes to almost 10 to read a given profile, but allow time to let your imagination wander where it will as you read ("I wonder if that policy could work here?" "How would I like working there?"). It is best to read the book a little at a time. Although they do not require much concentration and are very well written, the profiles begin to blur when too many are read in one session.

Ordering Information:	Addison-Wesley Reading, Massachusetts 01867
Call:	(617) 944-3700
Specify:	ISBN 0-201-15774-8
Price:	$17.95

Managing

Harold Geneen, with *Alvin Moscow*

Doubleday

© 1984
297 pages

Evaluation: More a treatise on managing by the former chief of ITT than an autobiography or a corporate history. The central question still remains: Is managing Geneen style something anyone but Geneen could or should do?

Thesis: Management is an emotional commitment to solving problems and achieving high standards. It requires the tenacity to demand reliable information in order to make correct decisions. A manager is defined by performance.

Audience: For any manager or any student of business; Geneen's system should at least be met in its pure form, even if not adopted whole.

Reading Time: 6 to 8 hours.

Authors

Harold Geneen is past chief executive officer and chairman of the board of the International Telephone and Telegraph Company (ITT). He is now chairman emeritus and a consultant for a venture capital firm.

Alvin Moscow is a professional writer. His books include *Collision Course* and *The Rockefeller Inheritance.*

Audience and Intentions

Managing is deceptively simple, and its deception and simplicity are both by design. That does not mean the book should be abandoned because it is dishonest; because it is not. It does mean that the book is much more revealing if we recognize all that is going on. Part of the virtuosity of **Managing** comes from having both a main author (Geneen) and a collaborator (Moscow). Consider, for instance, that we can identify four premises behind the book and four corresponding purposes.

The first premise-purpose pair is articulated by Geneen in his preface. Here he says that it is ordinary people who accomplish great things in the creative world of business during their "peak experiences." Geneen, as a self-described ordinary man of business now in the twilight of a long career, wishes to pass along "one or two basic truths" to others, "with the hope that they may engender some enlightenment."

The second set is spelled out by Moscow in his introduction to the book. Moscow relates Geneen's astounding accomplishments with ITT and chronicles the successes of his subordinates who went on to manage other firms. Geneen is here defined as the great teacher, and his book offers us an opportunity to enroll at "Geneen University." More than just business courses are available at GU, Moscow tells us: Geneen's "principles of good business management apply to aspects of all our lives. They have an astonishing universality." Geneen will also endorse this purpose at the end of chapter 1, but as an ordinary man of business he is less pretentious: "I am prepared to give you a complete course in business management. I can do it in just three sentences...."

The three sentences, as they will, grow into 12 chapters. While summing up the lessons of his course in chapter 13, Geneen reveals that there is some urgency to his teaching. "...As I look around, I see—as others do—American preeminence in business being overtaken by other countries. I get the impression that big business...is now befuddled and bewildered. I see what I consider mediocre performance all around me...." The third purpose, thus, is to save American business. "I care. That's why this book was written."

Finally, there is the hidden agenda that is evident, from the comments of both authors, to anyone familiar with business literature of the past few years. Geneen was once the most revered of all U.S. managers. Recently, however, the success of Japanese companies and our fascination with their management practices have cast his methods in an unfavorable light. Geneen, in fact, has become symbolic of old-time executives destructively obsessed with the bottom line. It would not be unkind to suggest that Geneen would be impelled to interpret his managerial techniques in a way, should we say, that reflects a healthier glow. That is his right certainly and even, considering his stature, an obligation.

Who then is the audience for this complicated-simple declaration of "one or two basic truths"? Anyone with the right frame of mind, the authors claim. Geneen dedicates the book "to all those who aspire, in whatever endeavor, to rise above the level of mediocrity." Moscow thinks anyone with an open mind should feel fortunate, as he does, to share a portion of "practical wisdom" from "the old master." In fact, any student of business or any manager might well be interested in Geneen's thoughts on managing.

Summary

Chapter 1: Theory G on Management (14 pages)

Theory G says that "you cannot run a business, or anything else, on a theory." During his career Geneen has absorbed dozens of theories, but none really worked as advertised, although fragments could be carefully applied. The current popular fascination with Japanese management is just a fad and no more relevant than Theory Y, or Theory X, or the scientific management phases we've been through before. In actual practice, decisions are made by people of character, leaders with the self-confidence to trust their abilities, not in accordance with a theoretical formulation.

In fact, the best way to run a business is to do it as you would cook on a wood-burning stove. Because you cannot control all the elements of the environment (wood, fire, air flow, etc.), you keep your eye on everything at all times. You adapt the recipes, taste, and make adjustments as you go along.

Chapter 2: How to Run a Business (15 pages)

Geneen's three-sentence course on business management is as follows: "You read a book from the beginning to the end. You run a business the opposite way. You start with the end, and then you do everything you must to reach it."

The success of a business is measured by performance over an extended period of time. At ITT, Geneen defined that performance as 10 percent or more yearly growth; that was the "bottom line." In order to reach that "end" objective, several intermediate goals had to be achieved in sequence. First the company had to be restructured, and then the management team overhauled. To attract top managers, generous financial incentives had to be put into place. And so on.

The same principle of deciding what you want to do and then start doing it applies to planning practices as well. Don't concentrate on five years down the road at the expense of immediate performance. You won't even make your yearly goals if you don't make the projections for the current quarterly earnings. If, on the other hand, you make the first three quarters, the fourth will take care of itself.

Chapter 3: Experience and Cash (28 pages)

"Experience is a process of discovering and learning something new, which somehow leads to a growing cumulative capability." Experience is what allows you to get into the top 20 percent of the people in your field and thus withstand downturns and earn more experience—all of which eventually leads to financial rewards. But the cash is secondary to the experience in value as well—the challenge and self-fulfillment comes from just doing the job.

Geneen built a diverse structure of life and career experiences on his road to ITT. He was born in England to an entrepreneurial father and an actress mother but educated in New England boarding schools. He applied his lessons of self-reliance and hard work to early jobs selling advertisements and clerking at the New York Stock Exchange while attending accountancy classes at night school during the Great Depression. He worked as a public accountant and then as a manager for American Can during World War II. Geneen was also a financial officer for first Bell & Howell, then Jones & Laughlin steel company, and finally Raytheon Company before taking over ITT at the end of 1958.

Chapter 4: Two Organizational Structures (21 pages)

The two organizational structures are the formal organizational chart and the informal network of daily relationships between people. The formal structure and chain of command are necessary to avoid chaos, but they put limits on what people can do and restrict the flow of information to the CEO. The boss cannot perform the central function of management—which is to actively manage—without the information necessary to make decisions.

ITT managed with open communications, comptrollers' reports, and monthly profit center reports. They managed this wealth of information with extra hard work and extra-long and vigorous General Managers Meetings. Their basic policy was "no surprises"—so all problems were red-flagged in advance and attacked by the entire staff as needed. Good, reliable information allowed the company to take calculated risks and reap the benefits thereof.

Chapter 5: Management Must Manage (19 pages)

"Management must manage" is an activist credo with strict performance criteria. It means that your budget and business plan are not something to shoot for, they are standards that *must* be achieved. If you don't achieve them you are not a manager. Managers get results; they do not accept explanations, no matter how reasonable. You get what you expect to get, so you must expect performance, whether in quality control or sales and earnings.

Management is not subjective; it can be measured every quarter by the profit and loss statement. To actually achieve results, you must be in control of your operations. You probe for problems and keep trying solutions until something works. You don't have to be perfect, but you do have to be better than your competition. If you can't do it, change the environment. The only thing you don't do is accept inadequate results and explanations.

Chapter 6: Leadership (20 pages)

Unlike management, leadership is purely subjective; it cannot be objectively measured. Leadership is the ability to inspire other people to work together as a team to attain a common objective. Leadership cannot be taught, but it can be learned through experience.

Geneen's leadership style was instinctive. His goal was to invigorate people at ITT and create a climate of growth and opportunity. To attract good people with enthusiasm and strong work habits, ITT paid higher than scale and offered performance bonuses; they also established open and honest communications. Those that couldn't take the heat were forced out of the kitchen—and that was appreciated by those who wanted to stay. Geneen also fostered imagination and creativity by allowing managers to take risks and make mistakes. He would in no case, however, tolerate a cover-up.

People don't work *for* their CEO; they work *with* him *for themselves*. Good CEOs are thus leaders, not commanders who rule by fear.

Chapter 7: The Cluttered-Desk Executive (13 pages)

Graduates of business schools have learned to shape their images in various ways, but the condition of their desks gives them away. The clean desk is not the emblem of an organized mind; rather, it is a sign that the executive is too far removed from the details of running his company. An executive who delegates too much responsibility can not correct a problem if things go wrong; he also runs the risk of becoming superfluous when things go right.

The corollary to the cluttered desk is the meeting that won't stick to an agenda and always runs late. Executives with clean desks and tight meetings also have inflexible appointment schedules. They think like all other super-organized business school graduates and so never get a jump on the competition. It is their mindset that is dangerous. They have unwarranted self-confidence and the fallacious belief that the future will fit their long-range plans.

Chapter 8: Not Alcoholism—Egotism (14 pages)

The cost of alcoholism can be measured in the billions of dollars each year. Alcoholism results in lost productivity, increased use of health and welfare benefits, bad management decisions, missed opportunities, poor morale, and high job turnover. ITT runs a model employee assistance program that has helped 89 percent of enrollees rehabilitate themselves and return to work.

As bad as alcoholism is, the worst disease affecting the work of business executives is egotism. While it does not injure the health of the individual, it is dangerous to the well-being of the company. And it is still in the closet. An egotistical executive has more than just normal pride; he is blind to reality, obsessed with image and perks, and eager for public recognition outside the arena of his job responsibilities. Because he has lost his common sense and objectivity, his decision-making process is warped. Egotism is difficult to deal with because it is not recognized as a disease. Many employees wind up manipulating self-obsessed bosses and resenting them.

Chapter 9: The Numbers (16 pages)

Many people mistakenly believe that large U.S. corporations like ITT are run heartlessly by the numbers. However, numbers are not the real business; they are pictures of the business. The more precise they are, the better they can tell management what is really going on. When managers learn to read numbers—a valuable skill acquired through extensive practice—they can locate significant variations between expectations and actual performance in the marketplace. The numbers won't tell a manager what to do, but they will signal a need for action. The key issue in business is to find out what is happening behind those numbers.

CEOs must insist on accurate numbers. Most business turnarounds occur when the new chief demands better quality, that is, better financial controls. Thousands of companies go bankrupt and hundreds more are taken over because management did not pay attention to the appropriate numbers. Paying attention to numbers is a drudgery, but comprehension of what the numbers mean will set you free. They will help you master the business.

Chapter 10: Acquisitions and Growth (26 pages)

Conglomerates came into vogue in the late 1960s and early 1970s when the rising stock market made many companies attractive buys. The public came to suspect conglomerates and infuse them, in their uneasiness, with evil intent. In fact, a conglomerate is merely a diversified company, with a central management, that produces a variety of products and services in more than one industry. It will prosper or fail depending on how well it is managed, just like any other company.

ITT emerged as a giant conglomerate in this period because that was the only path to growth. Most of the company's profits were generated overseas, and much of that business was vulnerable because countries in Latin America took over ITT-run phone systems with little or no compensation. Because telecommunications in the domestic market was regulated at the time, ITT looked elsewhere for acquisitions. They sought companies with future potential whose value could be enhanced by ITT ownership. Takeovers and mergers were always friendly, and most acquired businesses eventually became profitable in time.

Chapter 11: Entrepreneurial Spirit (19 pages)

There are no corporate entrepreneurs. Entrepreneurs are risk takers. They must be in business for themselves and be able to bet their whole company. Managers of large public corporations, on the other hand, are mistake avoiders. Nor do the stockholders want them to bet the company, even on the prospect of extraordinary gains. The exception to this rule might be Lee Iacocca at Chrysler; but he really had no choice. The same was true in ITT's early years under Geneen. As time went by and the company grew, however, the live-or-die risks were no longer appropriate, or perhaps even possible.

The structure of large corporations will not permit true entrepreneurs the freedom they really need. Salesmen and R&D inventors may come close, but they really don't fit the definition. Would-be entrepreneurs in corporate life must eventually leave to start a business of their own—or run an existing one that is floundering for lack of direction or energy—where they can take all the risks and reap all the rewards.

Chapter 12: The Board of Directors (18 pages)

Approximately 95 percent of the boards of directors are unable and unwilling to do their jobs, namely: represent and advocate the interests of the stockholders. They cannot judge the effectiveness of the chief executive because the CEO is their only source of information. In fact, he is usually on the board and is often the chairman.

In order for the board to function as it should it must obtain independent information to check on the accuracy of what management reports. The CEO would continue to attend meetings, but he and all other insiders would be removed from the board itself. The CEO would, of course, continue to run the company. This system would instill some real accountability. It should also make business more productive.

Chapter 13: On Caring: A Summing Up (13 pages)

Management is an emotional attitude, a living force that gets things done to an acceptably high standard. It involves staying on the job as many hours as it takes to find satisfactory answers to problems. That persistence will be emulated by subordinates until it becomes a way of life in the corporation.

The test of management is performance: whether or not sufficiently high goals have been achieved. And in order to accomplish those objectives, a manager must get reliable information necessary to make good decisions. To get good data he must do his homework and persistently ask the tough questions. If he succeeds he will have the leadership ability to help others succeed, which will create a momentum to make the enterprise thrive.

Chapter 14: Envoi!* (1 page)

Performance is the only reality in business. A manager is defined as the one who turns in the performance. Everything else can be, and will be, forgotten.

* * *

The book has a short index but no references, bibliography, or source notes of any kind.

Evaluation

Presentation

Most of the chapters adhere to the same basic structure: an epigraph from professor Geneen encapsulating the major theme, two or three pages defining that theme, an explication of the main and related ideas using Geneen's experiences at ITT as illustrations, and a redefinition of the main idea incorporating the words of the opening epigraph. It is an effective teaching approach. Chapters 3 and 10, the longest in the book, deviate slightly. The first is concerned with Geneen's life prior to ITT; the second surveys the history of ITT during the Geneen years. Both, however, are still more lesson-oriented than biographical.

The tone and style of **Managing** reflects Geneen's personality. The presentation is direct, abrupt, opinionated, intense, and fast paced. There is sparse use of metaphors and analogies, and those are all sports related. The book is clearly and efficiently written. There are occasional attempts at a more friendly, conversational—even avuncular—style, but these are about as convincing as a high-ranking Russian leader on a "good will" trip abroad. The book is too self-assured, too opinionated, and too tough minded to be charming.

All books try to manipulate our thinking, that is, to persuade us directly and/or indirectly that their truths are valid. **Managing** is

*Envoi: the explanatory or commendatory remarks to a poem, essay, or book.

crafted to appear natural and reasonable. It is only semi-successful—in part, because it tries too hard, in part (as we shall see below), because it is an unnecessary effort.

Content

The trouble is Geneen. He knows he is a real person with a complex, multifaceted personality, just like the rest of us. Unfortunately, whether through fate, circumstance, or connivance, the outside world insists on making him larger than life. Even his co-author contributes to the situation with his introduction. Moscow wants us to see Geneen as the great practicing teacher of management. Geneen projects himself as the down-to-earth, ordinary business man, whose few simple truths have been misunderstood or misrepresented over the years.

Both are fighting against Geneen's monumental public reputation. He was glorified as super manager in the 1960s and early 1970s, the symbol of powerful American management. That symbol took on a different aspect in the early 1980s when a totally different style of doing business seemed to be required for success in a new environment. In *The Art of Japanese Management* (Simon and Schuster, 1981), Pascale and Athos featured Geneen as "an archetype of a certain type of American boss" obsessed with his company's bottom line and contrasted him with the archetypal Japanese manager who had a more humane and socially concerned orientation.

Incredibly, their portrayal of Geneen's methods was not only accurate but fair. It matches Geneen's description in **Managing** perfectly. Only the interpretations are different. Geneen's system is complete and internally consistent. And everyone admits that it worked. Pascale and Athos contend that it could only work for an extraordinary individual like Geneen; they assert, in fact, that the system broke down in his absence. Moscow and Geneen say the methods work if applied with enough energy by any competent manager. That is why **Managing** depicts Geneen as both the great teacher (his lessons *can* be learned) and the ordinary man of business (they can be learned by *anyone*). At the same time, they can't separate the methods from the manager completely because ITT's performance under Geneen is what sells the system.

And there is more. Geneen is not only a symbol; he is an art form. Any attempt to dilute his purity is doomed to failure. Consider first one of his more famous memos, as reproduced in **Managing** (p. 97):

> The highest art of professional management requires the literal ability to "smell" a "real fact" from all others—and moreover to have the temerity, intellectual curiosity, guts and/or plain impoliteness, if necessary, to be *sure* what you have is indeed what we will call an "unshakeable fact."

Next consider this well-known passage:

> Now, what I want is, Facts. Teach these boys and girls nothing but Facts. Facts alone are wanted in life. Plant nothing else, and root out everything else. You can only form the minds of reasoning animals upon facts; nothing else will ever be of any service to them.

This bit of educational philosophy comes from Thomas Gradgrind, a character in Charles Dickens' novel *Hard Times*, published in 1854, approximately 100 years before Geneen's memo.

Geneen is certainly not the same as Dickens' caricature of the purely abstract man. Nor is he a calculating machine devoid of human feeling, or even a nineteenth century anachronism. It is, however, easy to see him as sadly out of date. His devotion to performance-only criteria evokes the kind of football coach mentality we used to admire 15 to 20 years ago in ITT's glory days. We were fond then of quoting Vince Lombardi's famous line: "Winning isn't everything, it's the only thing." Now we're a little embarrassed by the ruthlessness implicit in that statement.

That quote has also been interpreted as an unswerving striving for excellence, translating "winning" quite broadly. Excellence, of course, is rather a fashionable goal now. In fact, what Lombardi actually said was: "Winning isn't everything, but *wanting* to win is" (italics added). That comes much closer to the "emotional attitude" or "living force" Geneen describes as the essence of managerial success. Performance is the product of hard work.

The trouble, to repeat, is Geneen. It is so hard to separate the man from his message. Our opinion is that **Managing** would have been better off if Moscow-Geneen hadn't tried to shape his image. In the words of Bill Murray, "it just doesn't matter." What does matter is his managerial method. Ultimately, each individual reader will have to decide if Geneen and Moscow or Pascale and Athos are correct about the appropriateness of those techniques outside their original context. One might conclude—as Geneen does with other theories—that fragments of "Theory G" are worth adopting. In any case, we can cut through the "who-is-the-real-Geneen?" tangle and appreciate him and his system as a work of art done in the business medium.

Reading Suggestions

Managing is pleasant and engaging reading that does not require enormous concentration. Break up your reading in any manner that fits your schedule or interest. You might as well skip the book's introduction.

We do suggest that you read the chapter in *The Art of Japanese Management* (still available in some bookstores and in your local library) that analyzes Geneen, either before or after reading **Managing**. The two together present a more balanced picture. It seems to us that Moscow and Geneen may actually have structured their book in response to Pascale and Athos' treatment.

Ordering Information:	Doubleday & Company, Inc. Garden City, New York 11530
Call:	(516) 294-4400
Specify:	ISBN 0-385-17496-9
Price:	$17.95

The Organized Executive: A Program for Productivity: New Ways to Manage Time, Paper, and People

Stephanie Winston

Warner

© 1983/1985*
345 pages

Evaluation: A superbly organized and easily accessible guide to increased personal and professional productivity through more efficient management of paperwork, time, tasks, and staff functions. The advice is specific, practical, and of value to any manager—even a well-organized one.

Thesis: Applying the principles of good organization can reduce the personal confusion and the loss of productivity that result from managerial disorder.

Audience: For managers at all levels, but particularly top executives.

Reading Time: 5 to 7 hours.

*Our review copy was the 1985 Warner paperback. The book was originally published in 1983 by W.W. Norton & Company, Inc., 500 Fifth Avenue, New York, New York 10110.

Author

Stephanie Winston is president of a management consulting firm. She specializes in advising corporations how to increase managerial productivity through personal and systemwide organization. Ms. Winston is also the author of *Getting Organized.*

Audience and Intentions

Winston describes her book as the "distillation" of her clients' experience. She explains that her firm's consulting practice "relating to managerial productivity has made it possible to pinpoint the specific areas in which organizing is crucial and to recognize the steps toward effective management in a variety of situations, whether personal or professional."

The author thus calls upon what she has learned to answer two kinds of questions in **The Organized Executive**. The first she describes as "nuts-and-bolts" questions of a "how-to" nature concerning such daily chores as scheduling, paperwork control, filing, and time management. The second "fundamental" question of long-term productivity "involves practicing and changing habits" and confronting the "issue" of "personal values."

Consequently, **The Organized Executive** is intended to achieve three purposes. First, in responding to the "how-to" questions, it is a "straightforward reference." Second, and more fundamentally, it "explains why many managers feel out of control and the basic attitudes contributing to this perception." Third, in the same vein, the book "offers new ways to think about time, paper, and people so that potential productivity can be translated into a coherent program."

Winston presents an "Organizing Audit" in chapter 1 to help readers determine the "reorganizing program"—constructed out of various sections of the book—that will fit their needs. She contends that even well-organized people can benefit from the "tips" offered in subsequent chapters. She has, it seems, a program for every manager's state of chaos.

Summary

Chapter 1: The Organizing Principle (15 pages)

Managerial disorder costs companies significant sums in lost productivity dollars. A $50,000-a-year executive who loses one hour a day to poor organization costs the firm $6,000 annually plus opportunities missed due to inefficiency. In addition, managers suffer personally when disorder robs them of their confidence and blunts their competence.

Organization is not the same as neatness, nor does it mean surrender to a mechanistic behavior. Organizing is a learned skill by which to arrange time and workload to meet goals. It allows managers to be in command of their environment.

Part I: Paperwork

Chapter 2: The Paperwork Crisis: A Solution in Five Stages (26 pages)

Paper mismanagement can cripple a manager's ability to function effectively. The key to paper management is processing: channeling each piece to its appropriate destination.

The paper build-up can be curtailed with a five-step process. (1) Sort incoming papers through the TRAF system: *T*oss papers of no value; *R*efer papers to your secretary or staffers when they can handle them; *A*ct on papers requiring a response from you; *F*ile papers that might have future value. (2) If you process the mail with your secretary, turn back most papers to her with instructions for action. (3) If you do your own processing, schedule an hour a day for paperwork. (4) Keep track of complex, deferred, and referred actions with a calendar or tickler file. (5) At the end of each day, check your desk to make sure all papers have been TRAFed.

Chapter 3: Streamlining Paper: Shortcuts for Overload (21 pages)

Even when handled efficiently, the sheer quantity of paper flowing in and out of many offices remains a serious problem. It is possible, however, to reduce the volume by streamlining and standardizing many procedures.

Begin by evaluating reports. Collect a month's worth of reports and see if you can eliminate yourself from the routing list, have your secretary or assistant handle any of them, or, if necessary, have someone summarize them for you. Also try to eliminate or consolidate reports you generate. Reduce the number of people seeing the report, highlight key items, and simplify the text.

Form letters and "mix-and-match" letters with standard paragraphs can also reduce paper flow. Reading can be organized by discontinuing some subscriptions, skimming headlines, TRAFing all articles, creating a reading folder, and scheduling specific reading sessions.

Chapter 4: The Fine Art of Filing (29 pages)

Filing is more than a clerical chore; it is also a conceptual act of classifying information into usable categories. If you have easy access to information, you have an important resource at hand. An effective filing system can be constructed in a four-step program.

(1) Label each file according to its function or purpose. Labels should be broad, simple nouns. (2) Reorganize by working through each folder to discard obsolete materials; cross-reference; categorize as active, inactive, or referred; and mark an expiration or storage date on each item. (3) Block the system by placing files in convenient areas, having fresh labels and the file index typed, and reviewing equipment needs. (4) Maintain by assigning a file monitor, auditing regularly, and establishing filing policies.

Part II: Time and Task Management

Chapter 5: Shaping Your Workday: Crisis Management or Cool Control (25 pages)

The pressures of the daily demands of office life force many managers to lose sight of the larger picture. They can regain perspective by practicing "selective control": harnessing the time that can be controlled and minimizing the impacts of demands that cannot be controlled. They should begin by following the five action steps to increased productivity.

(1) Create a "Master List" by recording *every* idea, project, or task, of any size, as it arises. (2) Review the Master List daily to eliminate and delegate where possible. Enter deferred tasks on a calendar and jobs that must be done immediately on a "Daily List." (3) Compile tomorrow's ten-item "Daily List" from undeleted items on the Master List and your calendar. Rank each item either 1, 2, or 3 depending on priority and level of difficulty. (4) Try to enter more high-payoff tasks and fewer low-payoff tasks on the Daily List. (5) Schedule high-priority tasks for your best working ("prime") time.

Chapter 6: Mastering the Timewasters (25 pages)

It is possible and necessary to defend your schedule against timewasters: interruptions, meetings, and travel. Since you can't eliminate real emergencies, control prime time, private work periods, and scheduled appointments—and deal with the rest of the day more flexibly. Limit avoidable distractions and reduce the time spent on unavoidable ones.

The first line of defense is to adopt anti-interruption strategies to thwart unscheduled calls and visitors. Have your secretary screen incoming people and messages, consolidate visitors' time and call-backs, and schedule a "quiet hour." The second line of defense involves diagnosing problem interruptions. Redirect routine calls and brief staffers fully to anticipate inquiries. Third, streamline meetings by setting time limits and clarifying assignments. Finally, make business travel more efficient by preplanning your trip and preparing the office for operation in your absence.

Chapter 7: Efficiency and Your Work Profile (20 pages)

The key to time management is combining effectiveness (doing the right job) with efficiency (doing the job right). Many managers lose time to self-sabotage in the form of procrastination, perfectionism, and inefficient work style. The solution involves unlearning counterproductive habits.

Specifically, procrastination can be overcome by delegating disliked tasks, breaking jobs into simpler steps, building in intermediate completion points that will provide some gratification, and making arbitrary starts to overcome inertia. Perfectionism is a compulsive striving for an ideal far beyond any utilitarian purpose. Managers must learn to gauge the point of diminishing returns. Finally, shape an appropriate work style by first analyzing your favored approaches to tasks and then adopting strategies to schedule your job to best advantage.

Chapter 8: Project Management (20 pages)

A project is any highly complex task that involves numerous subtasks, intricate scheduling, and complicated monitoring techniques. Project management requires the formal organization of seven stages, although execution will depend on the sophistication and magnitude of the tasks.

(1) Set a specific goal. (2) Set a final deadline. (3) Break the project into subtasks. For unusually broad or abstract projects, first identify the underlying issues. (4) Organize subtasks into either sequential or parallel lines of development. (5) Set subdeadlines for individual tasks and establish periodic benchmarks for evaluating progress. (6) Delegate specific tasks to subordinates or outside consultants; enter your tasks on your Master List and Daily List. (7) Monitor tasks with calendars, tickler files, referral folders, task sheets, status reports, charts, and card files as appropriate for their complexity.

Chapter 9: Time Evaluation: From Objective to Reality (26 pages)

Getting organized is simply a means to an end. Time spent not getting where you want to go is time wasted. You can evaluate the "why" of time with three exercises: (1) "day-to-day analysis" of mastery of paperwork and time management, (2) "professional analysis" that identifies your own management-by-objectives (MBO) profile, and (3) "long-range analysis" that assesses whether you are on track for goals five or ten years in the future.

The first analysis involves logging each day's activities at 15-minute intervals and evaluating them for effectiveness according to the criteria established in this book. The MBO analysis entails defining two or three career objectives, choosing the two or three job components that offer the greatest payoff for you and your company, and then evaluating how well your present use of time squares with those objectives. The third analysis consists of envisioning a perfect day for yourself and translating the vision into concrete objectives.

Part III: The Art of Being a Boss

Chapter 10: Managing Staff (28 pages)

Personal organization of workload, papers, and time is part of a larger system that includes staff contributions as well. Productive managing requires orchestrating the skills and time of subordinates. Developing "human power" is essentially the process of effective delegation. The "cardinal rule of delegation" is to

> assign tasks to the most junior person who has the skills and rank necessary to complete the assignment successfully. If no one meets these criteria, find or train someone.

Symptoms of ineffective delegation include (1) frequent interruptions and inquiries from staffers, (2) need to redo substandard work, and (3) need to work late to catch up. Delegate responsibility for elements of complex tasks, routine tasks, first drafts, particular functions, and specific objectives. Consider tradeoffs with peers and the use of outside services or consultants. Be sure to define responsibilities, set priorities, provide necessary support, and follow up.

Chapter 11: On Secretaries: The "Team of Two" (27 pages)

Managers tend to underutilize the time and talents of potentially valuable associates. Many secretaries are capable of taking over complex tasks and thus enhancing both their effectiveness and that of their bosses. Secretarial duties fall into the categories of office supervision, "boss management," and independent projects. The key to building an effective partnership is to help your secretary expand these core functions to a higher level of responsibility requiring a higher level of initiative.

If you have your own executive secretary, you can outline and clarify those responsibilities. Meet daily to discuss assignments and solve problems. Shelter her time for priority work and keep yourself informed of her job progress and satisfaction. If you share a secretary, set up a work center on her desk to organize assignments from the various bosses. Clear any switch in priorities with your colleagues. If your company offers secretaries the option of becoming "administrative assistants," be sensitive to the psychological changes in status and functions such roles entail.

Chapter 12: Tools of the Trade: From Calculators to Computers (23 pages)

For many people, organization is synonymous with new equipment. Unfortunately, equipment itself can not organize you. Improperly used, it can aggravate a bad situation. Once internal systems are organized, however, the right hardware, applied correctly, can significantly increase productivity and efficiency. The key is matching the right tools. Executives should be aware of the uses and misuses of the most basic tools such as desk equipment and the electronic, technologically sophisticated machines such as word processors and computers. For the latter, a cost/benefit evaluation can be performed.

Schedules Appendix (10 pages)

The author provides examples of weekly work schedules, divided by day and hour, for nine of her clients.

Office Appendix (8 pages)

The author indicates the range of supplies needed for optimum office efficiency, evaluates selected pieces of equipment, and offers some notes on buying decisions.

* * *

The book's bibliography is arranged by topic; items consulted by the author are marked with an asterisk. Some entries are annotated. Winston recommends *all* entries for further reading. A few sources are also cited in the text or in footnotes. There is also an index.

Evaluation

Presentation

The Organized Executive is extremely well organized for productive use. The material is frequently arranged in lists, boxes, diagrams, charts, and "action steps" for ready accessibility. Each chapter concludes with a complete and concise summary. Winston includes several self-audits to focus readers' attention on their specific needs, and she makes frequent cross-references to related topics.

The book is also efficiently and effectively written. The advice is direct, nonthreatening, and encouraging. Winston's manner is matter-of-fact and self-assured. The tone is professional and neither too personal nor preachy. The very specific recommendations are illustrated by succinct and appropriate case histories.

Content

Disordered paperwork, poor time and task management, and inefficient staff organization undeniably cost businesses heavily. And, as Winston demonstrates, these productivity losses are avoidable. Winston offers a wealth of very specific, practical advice in an easy-to-use form. No matter what shape your office is in, she has a program to fit the need.

Furthermore, she has several self-evaluative instruments to help readers determine where to begin and what to do. If, after conducting the "Organizing Audit" in chapter 1, you conclude that you're in fine condition, you can still find several useful tips that could improve small problem areas or that suggest alternative practices. Executives with more serious organizational needs can follow the detailed program laid out in the first chapter and fine-tuned throughout the book.

As promised in her preface, Winston not only gives nuts-and-bolts solutions to organizational problems, she also instills a reassuring attitude of confidence. Her book makes it possible to believe that, by systematically applying the correct procedures, any manager can in time create order out of chaos.

Reading Suggestions

The obvious first step is to take the "Organizing Audit" in chapter 1 and follow the guidelines prescribed by the author. Her advice is specific, direct, and practical. You should also faithfully take all the additional audits for filing, time management, task efficiency, and so on, as they appear in the text.

We would add only two other suggestions. First, even though the summaries are very good, do not limit your reading to them. The chapters are full of useful recommendations that aren't included in the summaries. Second, don't try to read too much at one time; there is too much detail to assimilate. Probably the best approach is to organize your reading according to the major parts of the book.

Ordering Information:	Warner Books, Inc. 666 Fifth Avenue New York, New York 10103
Call:	(212) 484-2900
Specify:	ISBN 0-446-97755-1
Price:	$7.95

The World-Class Executive: How to Do Business Like a Pro Around the World

Neil Chesanow

Rawson Associates

© 1985
303 pages

Evaluation: A well-organized and concisely presented guide to international business negotiations that offers a great deal of practical and very specific advice applicable to many business and social situations in the major regions of the world.

Thesis: Successful business dealings abroad require executives to develop an understanding of other cultures and a sensitivity to the values of different peoples.

Audience: U.S.–based business travelers; businesspeople new to foreign travel; professionals anticipating the need to negotiate in foreign countries.

Reading Time: 8 to 9 hours.

Author

Neil Chesanow is a regular contributor of articles on business and travel to a number of publications. He is a former copywriter and advertising manager and the author of *Europe for One: A Complete Guide for Solo Travelers.*

Audience and Intentions

According to Chesanow, the domestic expertise of even a very competent U.S. executive is insufficient to "effectively negotiate elsewhere in the world...*even in Western Europe.*" In a "commercial world growing ever more interdependent" executives will have to develop both "international negotiating skills" and "cross-cultural awareness... to meet the ever-growing challenge of competition from abroad."

In **The World-Class Executive**, Chesanow thus sets out to detail "what non-Americans consider the *right* way to negotiate." He describes three basic types of non-Americans, including many national and regional variations, to help the reader "match an individual to his type to avoid causing offense and to effectively make your case" and offers insights, tips, and guidelines to provide "a definite negotiating edge over any competitor."

He defines his work as a book for doers, not thinkers. It is, he says, the "distilled essence," "bottom-line advice" that is practical, "short, and sweet." Chesanow draws on the experience of over one hundred experts for his recommendations. His scope is unusually broad. He deals comprehensively with Western Europe, the Arab World, East Asia, and Latin America and includes special tips for business*women* in each chapter.

The author identifies his audience as "U.S.–based business travelers who make short but frequent negotiating trips to foreign parts." The book is also for "executive expatriates," persons new to foreign travel, and even those who may be called upon to travel abroad for their firms in the future. In addition, it seems to us that **The World-Class Executive** could aid nontraveling CEOs in defining realistic expectations for their staff in foreign parts.

Summary

Part I: Us and Them

Chapter 1: What Makes You a Typical American (8 pages)

Negotiating blunders happen every day all over the world. They cost U.S. firms millions of dollars in lost contracts and deprive U.S. executives of raises, promotions, and even jobs. They occur because Americans act in a way that alienates foreign businesspeople—out of an innocent assumption that business practices are the same everywhere. Our foreign counterparts resent the typical American's money-based ethnocentrism, disinclination to attempt any language other than English, high-pressure style, preoccupation with time and deadlines, emphasis on profits over people, informality, obsession with talking shop, and lack of preparation.

Chapter 2: The Business World as One World (11 pages)

Experienced international negotiators have learned that (1) each of the world's businesspeoples is culturally unique, (2) beneath the differences there are often key similarities, and (3) the similarities are not the ones that Americans typically share. It is also possible to identify three types of non-Americans. The first is the strict cultural traditionalist who tries to preserve national identity. The second includes younger-generation people who have become Westernized or Americanized. The third—largest and fastest-growing faction—attempts a cultural compromise by blending old customs with modern ideas. Americans who wish to succeed in business in foreign countries must learn to recognize these types and their many variations and understand that each requires different treatment.

Chapter 3: Ground Rules for Getting the Goods (41 pages)

No matter where you go in the world, you can and should take advantage of the free expert advice available from experienced travelers in your own and other companies, international banks, trade publications, universities, federal agencies, foreign trade organizations, and foreign tourist offices. Once abroad, you will need patrons who can help you make appointments to see people and local representatives to continue your business initiatives. They should be true natives with good reputations.

Pre-negotiating trips are also useful for cultural background information. If that is impossible, try to arrive at your destination two or three days before your first scheduled appointment. It is also useful to try to learn a little of the language, hire the best interpreters and undergo cross-cultural training. You should know enough about local business and social rules to demonstrate that you're trying to be respectful, but don't try to "go native." Have all your written materials in both languages and use good quality printing. Both men and women should dress conservatively; the details are important. Gifts with the company logo are good, but not mandatory. They should not look cheap or be so expensive as to suggest a bribe. Finally, try to be flexible about your return home: things always take longer than you expect.

Part II: Strategies and Tactics

Chapter 4: Western Europe: The Civilization of Business
(39 pages)

For various reasons we have come to consider Europeans to be similar to ourselves, and, as a result, we expect their business methods and motivations to be similar as well. In fact, European executives are not like us. It is useful to think of Europe in three ways: (1) as a continent of fairly similar business cultures, (2) as a region of two broad-based cultures—the Germanic in the north and the Latin in the south, and (3) as a group of 30-odd countries with unique cultural identities.

Trust matters in European business; suspicion cancels out the desire to make money. Europeans are also characterized by conservatism, concern for social acceptance, formality, and lack of enthusiasm. Dress is conservative and tasteful. Put your academic degrees on your business cards, use formal address, and be prepared to shake hands a lot. Be punctual for appointments and concise in your presentations. Americans generally have the most trouble dealing with the French, more difficulties with the British than they anticipated, and fewer travails with the Germans and Dutch. All Europeans wish Americans had more civilized table manners and spoke more softly.

Chapter 5: A Thousand and One Arabian Nights (38 pages)

The commercial centers of the Arab world have been modernizing rapidly. Many Arabs are faced with making a cultural compromise between progress and ancient identities. They want Western technology, but fear the pollution of traditional values with Western ideas. Visiting business people will run the gamut of negotiators: from Bedouins to thoroughly internationalized Arabs. They must learn the common rules of etiquette in the Arab world without attempting the futile and patronizing task of "going Arab."

Westerners must also understand the basics of Islam, which influences every aspect of Arab life. Time, for instance, is a continuous flow, and deadlines are subject to the will of Allah. Arabs also give symbolic meaning to common acts of hospitality, which Westerners must reciprocate. Rules of decorum extend to dress, business appointments, greetings, gifts, written materials, and body language. Visitors must periodically reestablish good interpersonal rapport during business and social meetings.

Chapter 6: Getting Oriented (25 pages)

Oriental peoples are difficult to understand, but they are not beyond comprehension. The areas of East Asia considered here—Japan and the newly industrializing and rapidly modernizing countries of China, South Korea, Taiwan, Hong Kong, and Singapore—can be differentiated according to the degree in which the common heritage of Confucianism influences the way their peoples do business. Confucianism is an ancient ethical and civil code that propounds filial piety, kindness, righteousness, propriety, intelligence, and faithfulness. Stability and conformity are the basis of the system.

Because cultural outsiders are mistrusted, foreign business people must make a concerted effort to demonstrate respect and to understand the oriental point of view. Hierarchy, rank, and age are all important to oriental peoples—as is the subtle concept of "face," the omnipresent concern for status. To gain trust, Americans must be sincere, put people before profits, think in the long term, and respect cultural traditions as they apply to business and social meetings. Show patience, keep presentations low key, and leave the lawyers at home.

Chapter 7: Making It in Japan (36 pages)

Americans have more problems negotiating in Japan than any place else in the world. The failure-to-success ratio of 25 to 1 can be attributed to ignorance of Japanese culture; barriers to market entry are very seldom the cause. American firms mistakenly assume that Japanese and American needs are the same. But even cursory market research would reveal that Japanese consumers reject those Western goods that evidence uncompetitive pricing, improper specifications, and poor after-sale service.

To succeed in Japan, U.S. negotiators must respect Japanese methods and manners. The Japanese often choose, for instance, to be imprecise out of politeness and to preserve group harmony. Bring your own interpreter, but learn a little Japanese to make a good impression. Relationships between people are the basis for long-term commercial ties. Patience is needed for the Japanese process of decision making by consensus. In business meetings, the Japanese are distant and correct. They use social gatherings at *Karoke* bars to drink heavily and loosen up. Westerners should indulge within their limits to build trust, but they must be careful not to agree to anything they cannot live with in the cold reality of the next business day.

Chapter 8: Chinese Checkers (36 pages)

An emerging trading partner, the People's Republic of China (PRC), is a mystifying blend of old and new. The Chinese have a unique slant on international commerce. They study their Western counterparts, but lose any competitive edge to an inefficient bureaucracy and a political climate of rigidity, obtuseness, and paranoia. Communication between negotiators and decision makers is very poor, and it will be difficult to determine who has responsibility. Like the French, the Chinese not only feel superior to other cultures, they are conscious of, and even proud of, their ethnocentricity.

Negotiating successfully in China requires considerable patience and preliminary research. Business proposals should be factual, soft-sell, and aimed at a specific Chinese economic objective. Neither your clothes nor your gifts to your hosts should be flashy or too fashionable. Bring your CEO in, both to open and close negotiations; expect your technical people to be required to give seminars. Be aware of the several ploys the Chinese use to gain advantage in negotiations; they will extract promises and hold you to them. Watch out especially for the "mao-tai" (120-proof liquor) at the obligatory banquets.

Chapter 9: Selling in South Korea (17 pages)

Our predominant images of South Korea still come from *M*A*S*H* reruns and the Unification Church of Sun Myung Moon. However, in the past 20 years the country has become a significant industrial force and center of technology. South Korea is on the move, and, happily, its businesspeople are among the easiest in East Asia with whom to deal. A majority are adopting Western business practices, although a minority follow the Japanese model. The Japanese influence comes from several decades of cruel and total domination in the mid–twentieth century by that Asian neighbor.

Koreans, however, are known as the Irish of Asia. They are independent, individualistic, rough around the edges—by Asian standards—and easy for Americans to like. Saving face is not as important to modern Koreans, but it still influences negotiating behaviors. Westerners should have introductions by third parties, print business cards in both languages, and extend extra courtesy to older participants. Koreans tolerate more blunt presentations than other Asians and allow freer give and take. American firms would do well, however, to send cultured, soft-spoken representatives.

Chapter 10: Latins: The Other Americans (29 pages)

Even though Central and South America are characterized by economic and political instability, U.S. nationals can conduct successful business transactions if they understand the business cultures of the regions and are willing to make long-term commitments. They should also be aware that everyone in the western hemisphere is an "American" and that each country has a distinct personality of which it is very proud.

Many Latin businesspeople adopt some U.S. methods at the same time as they exhibit traditional traits of machismo, personalism, and the need to feel simpatico. Machismo is the exaggerated expression of masculinity; personalism is a more generalized concern with enhancing one's self-esteem. When these traits lead Latins to bare their souls to you, you must reciprocate—show your personality so that they may feel empathy (simpatico) and you can become compadres. The personal relationships you develop are far more critical than the professional ties between companies. Finally, be sensitive to the Latin's regard for hierarchy and rank, his fatalistic sense of time, and the seriousness of hospitality rituals.

Appendix: Where to Get Professional Help (3 pages)

The author provides the addresses and phone numbers of three national foreign language schools, five interpretation and translation services, and six cross-cultural training organizations. He also lists one book publisher and one producer of training films.

° ° °

Other than the general sources of information cited in the appendix and the "experts" listed in the acknowledgments, the book has no precise documentation—no bibliography, no footnotes. There is, however, an adequate index.

Evaluation

Presentation

The World-Class Executive is an exceptionally well-structured book. The text is divided into numerous short subsections. The organization of each chapter within both parts is similar if not identical. For the analyses of regions in part II, the breakdown is always: portrait of a businesspeople; business customs: dress, business cards, shaking hands, forms of address, appointments, collateral materials, presentation style, negotiating notes, decision-making process, lawyers and contracts, etc.; social customs: conversation, drinking, entertaining, gifts, etc. We are thus able to make comparisons between regions or countries with relative ease. The repetition that results from this standard structure reinforces the important lessons.

The writing is quickly paced, direct, and to the point. There is a good mixture of generalization and very specific advice. Unfortunately, there are few good anecdotes about doing business abroad, and several of these are familiar marketing horror stories. Typical of the tenor of the book is this bit of advice on appointments in Latin Europe:

> You may be kept waiting from a few minutes to over an hour in an outer office....Still, be punctual. It's expected that you sit and suffer. Don't leave and return later. Don't open your attaché case and find busy work to do. Simply sit. You must show a Latin that you respect the opportunity to meet with him....If you lose your temper, as many Americans do, you might as well stay home.

The World-Class Executive is thus not a particularly entertaining book, but it is certainly engaging.

Content

The World-Class Executive is a very serious book on the hard realities of international business negotiation. The process of negotiating includes more than bargaining across a table; there are social aspects and a cultural context to be considered. The strength of **The World-Class Executive** is its attempt to incorporate all these elements into a comprehensive whole for each major region of the globe and for selected countries. Chesanow explains how different peoples *think*, not just how they act. He elucidates the philosophy behind their behavior in a concise and insightful—though necessarily oversimplified—way. Even without the complexities and shades of gray, however, this approach provides an effective start toward understanding. For example:

> Just as there's a Muslim notion of fatalism regarding Arab time, so there is a Catholic concept of fatalism governing Latin time.... The American Puritan ethic dictates that through hard work deadlines can be met. But time is not money in Latin America.... Latins don't naturally believe that where there's a will there's a way. The only will that counts is God's. If something does not get done "on time," logic dictates that God's will overrules personal desire.

True to his theme of nonjudgmental understanding, Chesanow's objective commentary never suggests that any culture is intrinsically superior or inferior.

> The French rub people the wrong way. But then so do we, which is why, when Frenchmen and Americans try to negotiate, both often come away older but not wiser.

The value of the book comes from its clear but demanding formula for successful international negotiation: proper attitude plus proper attention to detail.[1] The proper attitude is an open-mindedness that permits cultural sensitivity and understanding. The details come from serious research into business and social customs. Chesanow provides more than a fair start with his host of very specific recommendations applicable to a wide range of situations in many geographical areas. His plea for cross-cultural understanding should be heeded by anyone expecting to venture beyond the U.S. borders—or, for that matter, for anyone dealing with ethnic domestic markets and populations.

Reading Suggestions

Even if you're convinced that your business will only take you to one sector of the globe, read the entire book—wide-ranging travel broadens the perceptions. Return to those chapters on specific locations as you need them. Further research will still be needed.[2]

[1]It sounds remarkably like Peters and Austin's equation for excellence. See review of *A Passion for Excellence*, also in this volume.

[2]We have reviewed a number of books with international themes. *Winning Back Your Market* (vol. 2, no. 5) and *Big Business Blunders* (vol. 2, no. 1) are especially relevant in this context.

Part I should be read as a unit; it will take less than two hours. Because of the wealth of information and advice in Part II, it should probably be digested a chapter at a time, although chapters 6–9 are all concerned with East Asia and should be considered as a unit.

Ordering Information:	Rawson Associates 115 Fifth Avenue New York, New York 10003
Call:	(212) 614-1300
Specify:	ISBN 0-89256-258-7
Price:	$16.95

Innovation and Entrepreneurship: Practice and Principles

Peter F. Drucker

Harper & Row

© 1985
277 pages

Evaluation: A book of unusual depth and perception that (1) defines the relationship of entrepreneurship and innovation to the economy and to society and (2) describes how to make these qualities part of the standard practice of management.

Thesis: Innovation and entrepreneurship are definable, concrete actions and behaviors that can be learned and systematically applied by individuals and institutions in the private and public sectors. Furthermore, if we view change as an opportunity, we can help create the entrepreneurial economy and the entrepreneurial society.

Audience: Decision makers and policy makers in all private businesses and public service institutions.

Reading Time: 8 to 9 hours.

Author

Peter F. Drucker is Clark Professor of Social Science at Claremont Graduate School in California. Dr. Drucker is one of the best-known writers on the management of modern organizations. His last two nonfiction books are *Managing in Turbulent Times* (1980) and *Toward the New Economics* (1981). His doctorate is in international law.

Audience and Intentions

In Drucker's judgment, other writings on innovation and entrepreneurship are misleading because they concentrate on the psychology and character traits of entrepreneurs and treat innovation as a slightly mysterious gift of inspiration or genius. This book differs "in both intention and execution." In it, Drucker presents innovation and entrepreneurship as "a practice and a discipline." He focuses on "the actions and behavior" of entrepreneurs; the case histories he relates exemplify points rather than just tell success stories. Drucker "represents innnovation and entrepreneurship as purposeful tasks that can be organized... and as systematic work," and he treats them "as part of the executive's job."

Drucker defines his latest volume as practical but not a "how-to." It deals with "such tangibles as policies and decisions; opportunities and risks; structures and strategies; staffing, compensation, and rewards." It presents the "knowledge base" of innovation and entrepreneurship "in an organized fashion," covering "the subject in its entirety and in systematic form." Nonetheless, Drucker considers it a "first book" rather than the "last word." He hopes it will be "accepted as a seminal book."

It seems that the author has two major goals. First, he wants to provide "concepts and tools" to make innovation and entrepreneurship "a normal ongoing, everyday activity, a practice in [management's] own work and in that of their organization." Second, he endeavors to define the relationship of innovation and entrepreneurship to the economy and to society. In Drucker's view, these concepts are applicable not just to new ventures but to established businesses and to public service institutions, which include schools and universities.

Innovation and Entrepreneurship is, consequently, for a wide range of readers. It is addressed to all thinkers and doers—policy makers and decision makers—in both the public and the private sectors.

Summary

Introduction: The Entrepreneurial Economy (17 pages)

The United States is shifting from a "managerial" economy to an "entrepreneurial" one. In the last decade, we have created more jobs than even in the 25-year period following World War II. Then the growth was in large institutions; now that sector is losing jobs—about as many as high tech is generating.

The popular Kondratieff theory of cyclic stagnation fails to explain an increase of 40 million jobs. They are coming from everywhere, but particularly in mid-size (revenues $25 million to $1 billion) companies. These firms are examples of the "new technology" of entrepreneurial management that applies knowledge to human work. This is sytematic, purposeful, managed entrepreneurship; it is innovation, rather than the invention and speculation of Silicon Valley. The causes are changes in values, attitudes, demographics, institutions, and behavior that promote a search for and exploitation of new opportunities. The need now is to formulate principles and practices to guide the development.

Part I: The Practice of Innovation

Chapter 1: Systematic Entrepreneurship (9 pages)

Entrepreneurship creates new markets and new customers; it changes values. Entrepreneurship is practiced by large and old enterprises as well as small and new ones, by public institutions as well as businesses. Whether in individuals or institutions, it is behavior founded on rational concepts rather than personality traits or intuition. Entrepreneurs see change as the norm and as healthy. Indeed, they are always searching for change to exploit it as an opportunity. Yet entrepreneurship is risky only when entrepreneurs don't know what they are doing. Entrepreneurship needs to be managed, and it needs to be based on purposeful innovation.

Chapter 2: Purposeful Innovation and the Seven Sources for Innovative Opportunity (7 pages)

Innovation creates resources or changes the wealth-producing potential of existing resources. It is thus an economic or social rather than a technical term. Systematic innovation consists of the purposeful and organized search for changes and the systematic analysis of the opportunities such changes might offer for economic or social innovation. It means monitoring seven sources for innovative opportunity: (1) the unexpected; (2) the incongruity; (3) innovation based on process need; (4) changes in industry or market structure; (5) demographics; (6) changes in perception, mood, and meaning; and (7) new knowledge.

Chapter 3: Source: The Unexpected (20 pages)

Unexpected success offers rich opportunities for successful innovation with few risks. Management, however, finds it difficult to believe in anything that contradicts familiar norms. Accepting unexpected success takes determination, a willingness to look at reality, and the humility to admit error. Unexpected success is a symptom; it must be analyzed to be exploited. It forces us to ask what opportunities it presents and what changes it will require. Above all, it demands seriousness and support on the part of management.

Similarly, unexpected failure also bespeaks underlying change, and, with it, opportunity. It should jolt us out of our assumptions and convictions. Unexpected events in a supplier's business, or a competitor's, or among customers are also signals to investigate because they represent the potential for innovation.

Chapter 4: Source: Incongruities (12 pages)

An incongruity is a discrepancy between what is and what ought to be. It creates an instability in which minor efforts can bring about economic restructuring. There are four basic areas of incongruity: (1) between the various economic realities of an industry, (2) between the reality of an industry and the assumptions about it, (3) between the efforts of an industry and the values and expectations of its customers, and (4) within the rhythm or the logic of a process. The innovation that exploits an incongruity should be small and simple, focused and highly specific.

Chapter 5: Source: Process Need (7 pages)

Innovations based on "process needs" perfect a self-contained process that already exists by replacing a weak link or redesigning the process around newly available knowledge. It is task oriented rather than situation oriented. There is a clear definition of the objective and of the specifications of the solution. There is also high receptivity: it is immediately accepted as "obvious" and soon becomes "standard."

Chapter 6: Source: Industry and Market Structures (12 pages)

Often industry and market structures appear so solid as to be part of the order of nature and certain to endure forever. Actually, they can disintegrate easily with change. All industry members must then ask themselves anew what the nature of their business is. Since insiders tend to view changes as threats, however, it is outsiders who can innovate if they are alert to the signals of impending change: (1) rapid growth of an industry, (2) convergence of technologies, and (3) changes in the way business is done. Innovations are particularly effective if the industry is dominated by one large manufacturer or supplier and if they are kept simple.

Chapter 7: Source: Demographics (11 pages)

Demographics are the changes in population size, age, structure, composition, employment, education, and income. They are unambiguous and have predictable consequences—that is, an impact on what will be bought, by whom, and in what quantities. Demographics are important because populations are unstable and subject to sudden sharp changes. Because demographics are neglected by managers and experts, entrepreneurs have opportunities to take advantage of altered conditions. They should be particularly aware of the demographic factors of age distribution, educational attainment, occupational segmentation, and income distribution.

Chapter 8: Source: Changes in Perception (8 pages)

When a change in perception takes place, the facts do not change, but their meaning does. The observer stops seeing a glass "half empty" and begins seeing it "half full," although the amount of liquid in the glass remains constant. The change can come very quickly—as when the majority of Americans began viewing themselves as "middle class" rather than "working class." Even if not quantifiable, perception changes can be tested, defined, and exploited. Timing is critical: innovations can be neither too late nor premature. In addition, innovations should start small and be very specific.

Chapter 9: Source: New Knowledge (23 pages)

Knowledge-based innovations need not be scientific or technical; social innovations can have equal or greater impact. Knowledge-based innovation is hard to manage. It differs in timespan, casualty rate, predictability, and challenges posed to the entrepreneur. It has, for instance, the longest lead time of all innovations: typically taking as much as 25 to 35 years to become applicable and begin to be accepted in the marketplace. Knowledge-based innovation also depends upon the convergence of several different kinds of knowledge, as with the computer.

It requires careful analysis of all necessary factors, a clear focus on strategic position, and the practice of entrepreneurial management. Even then, it is very risky because the window of opportunity is not open long and several entrants are trying to crowd through. In addition, the shakeout sets in as soon as the window closes.

Chapter 10: The Bright Idea (3 pages)

Even though innovations based on a bright idea outnumber all other categories taken together, they are the riskiest and least successful source of innovations. No one knows which ideas have a chance to succeed and which are likely to fail. Entrepreneurs are advised to forego innovations based on bright ideas despite the enticing success stories; they are like betting on hitting a jackpot on the slot machine.

Chapter 11: Principles of Innovation (8 pages)

Purposeful, systematic innovation begins with the analysis of the sources of opportunities. Because innovation is both conceptual and perceptual, innovators must go out and look at the needs and values of customers. Innovations must be simple and focused; they start small and try to do one specific thing. Innovators aim at leadership, which is not the same as becoming a big business.

Innovators should not try to be clever, attempt to do too many things at once, or focus on the future instead of the present. Innovation takes hard work. Innovators must build on their strengths and be market driven to produce an effect on the economy and society. Successful innovators are opportunity focused rather than risk focused.

Part II: The Practice of Entrepreneurship

Chapter 12: Entrepreneurial Management (4 pages)

Entrepreneurial management is a discipline that applies to the existing business, the public service institution, and the new venture. Today's businesses must acquire entrepreneurial competence to survive. Yet it is the existing business of fair size that has the best opportunity, capability, and responsibility for effective entrepreneurial management. Public service institutions, too, must adapt to change. Finally, new ventures will require the development of managerial skills to realize their potential for innovation.

Chapter 13: The Entrepreneurial Business (30 pages)

There are enough large companies doing well as entrepreneurs to disprove the notion that big businesses cannot innovate. Bigness is not an obstacle to entrepreneurship and innovation because those processes are not natural, creative, or spontaneous and thus necessarily thwarted by bureaucracy. They must, in fact, be striven for with great, disciplined effort.

Entrepreneurial management requires policies and practices in four major areas. (1) Organizations must be receptive to innovation and willing to perceive change as an opportunity rather than a threat. (2) Systematic measurement of a company's performance as an entrepreneur and innovator is necessary for improvement. (3) Specific practices must be established pertaining to organizational structure, staffing, and compensation. (4) Management should avoid mixing entrepreneurial units with the rest of the business, diversifying away from its field, and acquiring small entrepreneurial companies.

Chapter 14: Entrepreneurship in the Service Institution (11 pages)

Since the rapid changes in today's society, technology, and economy are an even greater threat to public service institutions, they need to be entrepreneurial and innovative. Unfortunately, stopping what has always been done and doing something new is very difficult. The service institution (1) is based on a budget rather than earned revenues, (2) is dependent on a multitude of constituents, and (3) exists to "do good." Thus its mission is a moral absolute not subject to economic cost/benefit analysis. The public service institution is out to maximize rather than optimize its impact.

To become entrepreneurial, it must focus its mission on clearly defined and realistic objectives instead of programs. Failure to meet these objectives should mean that they or their definitions are wrong. Hence, they must be changed—and the change must be viewed as an opportunity, not a threat.

Chapter 15: The New Venture (19 pages)

In order to survive, new ventures must develop into new businesses and be "managed." Entrepreneurial management of a new venture requires (1) a focus on the market, (2) financial foresight for cash flow and capital needs, (3) the building of a management team long before the new venture actually needs one and long before it can actually afford one, (4) a decision on the appropriate work role for the founding entrepreneur.

New ventures must operate on the assumption that their products or services may find customers in unexpected markets. Their managers must then be ready to experiment and be receptive to unexpected successes and failures. They also need to feed growth with profits. To build a management team, founders must build mutual trust and understanding with staff. They must think through their roles to arrive at the most significant contributions they can make once the business is established. Finally, the entrepreneur in the new venture needs independent, objective advice.

Part III: Entrepreneurial Strategies

Chapter 16: "Fustest with the Mostest" (11 pages)

In this strategy, the entrepreneur aims at leadership, if not at dominance, of a new market or a new industry. Being "fustest with the mostest" does not, however, necessarily mean becoming a big business. It is a risky approach but potentially very rewarding. Because the strategy has to hit right on target or it will miss altogether, it requires thought, careful analysis, and extreme concentration of effort. Innovation must continue to find new uses and new customers; prices have to be systematically cut to discourage competition. The extreme risks dictate that the strategy be used only with major innovations.

Chapter 17: "Hit Them Where They Ain't" (13 pages)

"Creative imitation" is the first of two substrategies. The entrepreneur offers a product or service that is adapted from someone else's innovation and that will really satisfy the customer. In a short time, the creative imitation sets the standard and takes over the market. The strategy exploits the success of the originator by supplying something that was lacking. It is less risky but still aims at market leadership. It is best suited to a major product in a rapidly growing market.

"Entrepreneurial judo" is the second substrategy. Here the entrepreneur analyzes the industry, identifying the bad habits of firms. The tendencies to arrogance ("not invented here"), to take the high-profit ("cream") of a market, to focus on what the producer rather than the customer believes is quality or value, to be deluded by the idea of "premium pricing," and to maximize rather than optimize make a company vulnerable to judo. Still, users must provide something distinctive that the market wants.

Chapter 18: Ecological Niches (10 pages)

This strategy aims at control rather than dominance; it seeks a practical monopoly in a small area. Here, entrepreneurs avoid bigness, visibility, and competition. Variations include the toll-gate strategy, the specialty skill strategy, and the specialty market strategy. In the first, the product is essential to a process, and the risk of not using it must be infinitely greater than the cost. The second comes from developing a high skill at a very early time in the industry's history. The third differs only in that it exploits a key market instead of supplying a key skill. Although the toll-gate is static and the special strategies are adaptive, all are very vulnerable to changes in the environment.

Chapter 19: Changing Values and Characteristics (10 pages)

In this instance, the strategy is the innovation because it converts an old, established product or service into something with new utility, value, or economic characteristics. The strategy creates customers by (1) creating utility, (2) pricing, (3) adapting to the customer's social and economic reality, or (4) delivering what represents true value to the customer. All variations focus on what the customer wants or believes rather than what the producer has grown accustomed to thinking is "right."

Conclusion: The Entrepreneurial Society (14 pages)

Whether they accomplish their objectives or not, all institutions, systems, and policies eventually outlive themselves. Innovation and entrepreneurship are thus needed in public service institutions as much as they are in businesses. They can keep the society flexible and self-renewing because they are pragmatic rather than dogmatic and modest rather than grandiose. To achieve this goal, executives of all institutions must make innovation and entrepreneurship a normal, ongoing, everyday activity.

As a society, we need to encourage continuous learning and the acceptance of change as an opportunity. This means rethinking our assumptions about schooling, taxes, governmental regulations, displaced workers, and social policies. We are at what could be a major turning point in history: the emergence of the entrepreneurial society.

* * *

Drucker concludes with a two-page "Selected Bibliography," in which he analyzes the merits of approximately one dozen books, articles, and reports. Most of the few source footnotes in the text refer to Drucker's earlier works. The author also provides an index.

Evaluation

Presentation

Peter Drucker's books have a special character; they are distinctive in ways other than those he mentions himself (see Audience and Intentions). Typically, **Innovation and Entrepreneurship** is intelligently presented, carefully thought out, and persuasive. Its tone is very straightforward and very confident. There is also a wonderful balance between concept (generalization) and case history (illustration).

The best quality of the book, however, is that it goes beyond the norm. The "founding father of the science of management"* writes from a historical and societal perspective to encompass more than management and business. The whole world is the natural subject of the entire text—in contrast to the standard management-book treatment, which is a "conceptual framework"

*A title originally given him by the *Los Angeles Times*.

with cosmic pretentions tacked on at the conclusion. **Innovation and Entrepreneurship** is excellent and rare social science.

Content

Drucker's latest effort is a book of ideas, designed to expand our horizons and focus our efforts. Both goals are the product of the author's comprehensive definition of innovation and entrepreneurship. The perspective, as we have indicated, is broadening: it shows that our economy is definitely evolving toward an entrepreneurial state and that our society has an achievable potential for doing so.

Drucker's perspective on innovation and entrepreneurship also explains how we might effectively advance the desired future in our business and public service institutions. He accomplishes this important task by defining innovation and entrepreneurship in such a way as to deliberately demystify and demythify them. No longer are they rather intangible qualities that are, in some inexplicable way, the province of a select smattering of unique people. Innovation and entrepreneurship are instead definable, concrete actions and behaviors that can be learned and systematically practiced by individuals and institutions in the private and public sectors as part of their normal, everyday business.

Innovation and Entrepreneurship thus provides the vision of economic and social possibility and the concepts and tools to enhance its development. It also describes the attitude or world view necessary to achieve these goals. We must, the book tells us, see change both as the norm and as an opportunity. The opportunities include, but are by no means limited to, business success.

Whether or not Drucker is correct that we are on the threshold of a new economic order and within sight of a new social one, his book offers many very useful insights for stimulating innovation and entrepreneurial management. His book is consequently of sure practical value and quite likely—as he hopes—a seminal work that should not be ignored.

Reading Suggestions

We have very little to add to the standard advice: (1) don't neglect the introduction and jump ahead to chapter 1 and (2) try to organize your reading according to the major parts. Part I is probably too long for one sitting, but we did find it the most interesting. You might skip the footnotes: they do not contribute directly to the argument.

Ordering Information:	Harper & Row 10 East 53rd Street New York, New York 10022
Call:	(212) 207-7000
Specify:	ISBN 0-06-015248-4
Price:	$19.95

Managing Corporate Culture

Stanley M. Davis

Ballinger

© 1984
123 pages

Evaluation: A tightly written book that provides a practical definition of corporate culture by distinguishing between guiding and daily beliefs, links culture to strategy with a cultural risk matrix, presents case histories of strategic cultural change, and offers a larger perspective on the power of such change.

Thesis: Corporate culture can be managed—and it should be managed well because of the crucial linkage between culture and strategy. Culture provides a sense of worth for employees, a purpose for the corporation, and a basis for ethical behavior.

Audience: For top executives, who hold the key to strategic cultural change; for lower-level managers who wish to persuade the CEO to act or to appreciate the concept.

Reading Time: 3 to 5 hours.

Author

Stanley M. Davis is a Massachusetts-based independent consultant, specializing in implementing strategy through management, organization, and culture. Dr. Davis has written several books on management and has been on the faculty at Boston University, Columbia, and Harvard.

Audience and Intentions

According to Davis, it was he who coined the term "corporate culture" in a book published in 1970, almost 10 years before it came into popular usage as a management concept. Even with all that has been published recently, Davis still believes that no one has "written a book about first-hand experience working with companies to manage and change their cultures." He considers the subject of culture to be "both complex and frequently misunderstood." His purpose, then, is to "share [what he has] learned about managing corporate cultures, and in the process, perhaps, to demystify the culture phenomenon," which organizations have been variously defining as "style," "identity," "philosophy," "purpose," "roots," and "vision."

In order to achieve a common perspective, Davis defines corporate culture as

> the pattern of shared beliefs and values that give the members of an institution meaning, and provide them with the rules for behavior in their organization.

He contends that corporate culture *can* be managed—and that such control is important because "the linkage between corporate culture and strategy is crucial." Within a larger context, Davis believes that culture provides a sense of worth for employees, a prescription for good health for the corporation, and a basis for ethical behavior.

Although the intended audience for **Managing Corporate Culture** is not explicitly identified, it is obviously directed toward top executives—because of the author's conviction that "nothing much happens to the culture if the CEO doesn't support a change effort." By implication, the book might also prove useful to lower-level managers wishing to energize their company or their boss.

Summary

Chapter 1: Cultural Realities (9 pages)

The current popularity of "culture" as a management concept results from a major search for new strategic models. Corporate culture is more flexible and less mechanistic than more traditional approaches; at the same time, it offers a return to fundamentals.

To determine a firm's culture, one must distinguish between guiding and daily beliefs. Guiding beliefs give direction to the company: they define how to compete and how to manage the organization. Daily beliefs are rules and feelings that govern everyday behavior.

Guiding beliefs are the motives that impel a company to accomplish its strategy: they are the precepts upon which strategies are formulated. Guiding beliefs are invariably set at the top and transmitted down through the ranks. Thus CEOs who, with the aid of a team of top managers, forge or reassert guiding beliefs to strengthen strategy are most likely to be effective.

Chapter 2: Capturing Beliefs (8 pages)

Expressing the beliefs of an organization in words is an elusive task, but the stories that senior executives tell about the company can provide a beginning. The morals of these stories will elucidate the guiding beliefs, as management perceives them. The plots will uncover the daily beliefs, which determine what helps or hinders the implementation of strategies.

"Cultural risk" can be determined by asking two questions: (1) How important is each action to the success of the strategy? and (2) How compatible is each action with the daily culture? The responses can then be plotted on a matrix divided into negligible, manageable, and unacceptable risks (see diagram).*

*From Davis' MANAGING CORPORATE CULTURE, Copyright 1984. The Human Resource Planning Society. Reprinted with permission from Ballinger Publishing Company.

Assessing Cultural Risk.

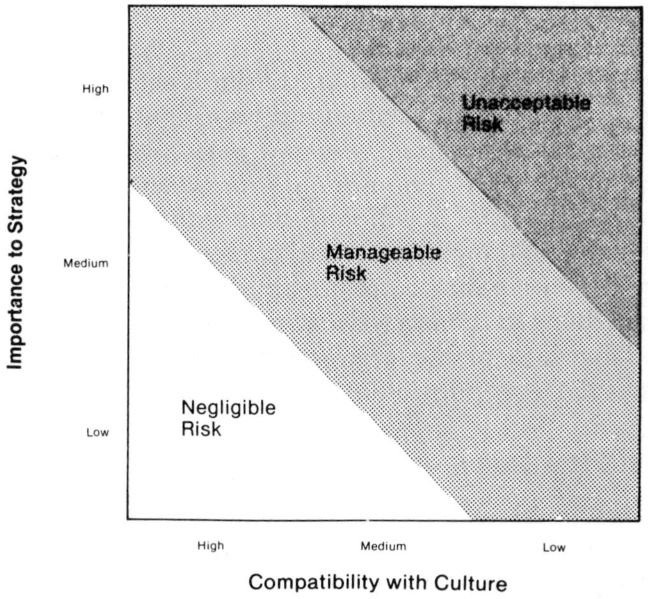

Answers to these two questions can reflect a consensus of a management workshop. This process identifies the major dangers to the implementation of strategy. It also forces managers to think about the relationship of a business plan to the organization that must carry it out.

Chapter 3: Turnaround at First Chicago (19 pages)

The story of the First National Bank of Chicago illustrates the benefits of a firm grasp of the relationship between culture and strategy. After a tumultuous decade in the 1970s, managers at First Chicago realized that they had lost their sense of what they stood for as an institution. Under the leadership of Barry Sullivan, they sought a definition of a corporate culture that they felt would help implement a newly articulated strategic vision.

They started by organizing the history of the bank into five major periods: (1) the early years of tranquillity from 1863 through the 1960s, (2) the period of rapid growth from 1969 to 1975,

(3) the troubled times of lost direction from 1975 to 1981, (4) the transitional period of 1981 to 1983 when they searched for an identity, and (5) the future culture in which the bank would become strategically driven.

Next, they reviewed five mainline business activities—international banking, customer relationship management, investment banking, management processes, and personnel policies—and plotted specific desired actions in those areas on the cultural risk matrix (see chapter 2). They did the same with key cultural issues such as decision making, tenure, and perspectives on customers.

The process of creating a culture appropriate to new external and internal demands generated a turnaround at First Chicago. It succeeded because of the commitment of the CEO and the members of the directing committee.

Chapter 4: Pitfalls (19 pages)

Managers should become familiar with the diagnosis, prevention, and correction of pitfalls common to attempted corporate culture change. Some of these are

- *The nonevent*—a change is announced with fanfare, but nothing ever happens, thus undercutting subsequent attempts. It can be prevented by taking a low-key approach and corrected by changing the focus from immediate benefits to an appreciation of the beliefs themselves.
- *Lip service*—mistaking the words for the thing itself. Get people to participate in and not just talk about change. Find different ways to describe the process.
- *Pleasing the boss*—moving only when the boss pushes. The yes-man syndrome is hard to prevent; it can be corrected only by rewarding constructive criticism.
- *Cynicism*—results when management can't demonstrate its stated beliefs. Don't espouse what you can't actually achieve. Cynicism can be cured by "cleaning the leaders' house or cleaning out the leaders."
- *Tail wagging the dog*—daily beliefs (rather than guiding beliefs) driving the strategy and actions; bureaucracy rules.

Prevention and correction both involve keeping the guiding beliefs out front. Focus on the positive effects of following the guiding beliefs rather than eliminating entrenched daily ones.

Chapter 5: What Happened at Harrison (20 pages)

The "Harrison" case illustrates what can happen to a firm when it fails to recognize common pitfalls. "Harrison" represents a composite of large, mature, product-built companies trying to compete in a systems-driven arena. Management is aware that it is drifting and that employees are cynical about the CEO's espousals of guiding beliefs, especially concerning strategic planning, customer service, and corporate citizenship. Dignity has yielded to arrogance, and the best people are trying to get out. Most have adopted a loser's view of the corporation and its culture.

Harrison made several organizational changes to address its performance problems. It developed a strategic planning effort, integrated the sales force, cut staff and costs, and initiated employee involvement programs. All of those actions can be plotted on the corporate risk matrix introduced in chapter 2. The analysis indicates that many cultural barriers will have to be overcome. Indications are that success will be hard to achieve.

Chapter 6: Daily Culture (13 pages)

When a company's daily culture diverges from its guiding beliefs, a credibility gap opens up. The greater the gap, the greater the cultural risk to strategy implementation. It is possible systematically to document the existence or absence of a credibility gap. One method is to gather information on how management tasks, such as decision making or communications, are carried out and how such organizational relationships, as between peers or between boss and subordinate, are formed. Another is to survey the climate of a company. A "good" climate exists when employees have adopted the values of the prevailing company culture.

Corporate systems for such purposes as planning or managing human resources should be checked to see if they support or undermine the guiding beliefs. If, for instance, you discover that in the area of career planning employees feel that moving outside the home unit is risky, then you know that this daily belief is at odds with the guiding belief of diversity. Consequently, the career progression system should be rebuilt.

When a strategy requires new behavior, executives have several options. They can ignore the culture, which is dangerous; they can manage around the culture by changing the implementation plan; they can change the strategy to fit the culture; or they can try to change the culture to fit the strategy.

Chapter 7: A Billion-Dollar Culture (25 pages)

Analog Devices, Inc., is attempting to meet the challenge of making the transition from a small, fast-growing firm to a major corporation. Corporate culture is the glue that can hold a company together in such times of stress and redefinition. Analog is blessed with a strong founder and leader, Ray Stata, who is transforming himself from an entrepreneurial engineer into a CEO. Analog's culture emanates from him.

Analog's culture can be defined by its beliefs about strategy, organization, subcultures, people, finance, and marketing and technology. The strategy is to let technological innovation define the business. The favored organizational mode is decentralization whenever possible; consequently, subcultures are formed and tolerated. Analog also believes in meeting the needs of employees and customers; it has a humanistic orientation toward self-actualization and trust. The company strives to remain self-financed. It wants to diversify its technological achievements into a variety of marketable products.

Analog's overwhelming guiding belief, however—the belief shared by all its people—is that the company is a winner, an industry leader. Analog people also believe that they are critical to the company's success, that they make a difference.

Chapter 8: Corporate Cultures in a Larger Context (5 pages)

Most people do not make the connection between their company's core values and beliefs and their everyday behavior.

There are, however, increasing numbers of business leaders who think that their employees' knowledge of what they stand for nurtures a corporation's roots. Culture, as an expression of purpose and ultimate meaning, provides the standard for ethical behavior by which a company and its leaders will be judged. Corporations with worthy purposes beyond financial returns can aspire to greatness. They provide an opportunity for people to make a contribution to something that is larger than themselves.

* * *

Managing Corporate Culture was constructed from the author's thoughts and experiences. It has no source notes, bibliography, or index.

Evaluation

Presentation

Davis writes in a sparse, assertive style of short, no-nonsense declarative sentences. The book is personal only in the use of direct address ("From my experience, I know you will need to..."). The presentation is precisely formulated and easy to follow in the conceptual chapters (1, 2, 4, and 6), although some parts of chapter 6 are a little murky. Most of the diagrams are clear and helpful—indeed, essential—the exceptions being the ones Davis borrows from other sources (again, in chapter 6).

The case histories that constitute chapters 3, 5, and 7 are analytical treatments designed to illustrate specific points; they have no storytelling character. In that regard, the book is more abstract than concrete. It is efficient, economical, and effective—but not intended as entertainment. Only when he praises the beautiful culture of Analog (chapter 7) or philosophizes on the larger importance of culture (chapter 8) does Davis's prose style really soar. The rest of the book is written in a workmanlike style: professional, spare, and lucid.

Content

Managing Corporate Culture is an excellent book with a good, simple conceptual framework that is both plausible and comprehensible. It is arguable, however, whether readers will get sufficient guidance from this small volume to apply its advice to their own work situations, although Samuel H. Armacost, CEO of the Bank of America and a client of Davis's, highly praises the utility of Davis's approach in his foreword.

Although **Managing Corporate Culture** does not provide step-by-step instructions, it does make a vital distinction between guiding beliefs and daily beliefs—the key components of culture—that should have considerable practical value for defining corporate culture and checking its consistency. Further, Davis provides a very useful management tool—the cultural risk matrix—by which to assess the cultural ramifications of particular strategic actions.

The book's second contribution of value is crystallized in the short concluding chapter. Here Davis explains why corporate culture is more than a management tool. He describes the incredible power of meaning, of belonging, of fundamental beliefs honestly held—and, conversely, the destructive force of hollow guiding beliefs, of manipulation, of loss of business purpose beyond the bottom line.

Managing Corporate Culture is a nicely polished little gem of a book. Its value should appreciate with wear.

Reading Suggestions

Samuel Armacost's foreword is an extremely valuable introduction to Davis's work: take a look at it before you begin chapter 1.

Davis's argument is not hard to follow, but don't yield to the temptation to read too quickly. He doesn't waste any words in extended explanations, and you could miss some key distinctions.

Because the case studies correspond to points made in preceding chapters, the natural breaks come after chapters 3, 5, and 7. Dividing the book into thirds (foreword through chapter 3, 4–5, 6–8) gives you three reading sessions of from one to one and a half hours each. However, given the good transitions between chapters and the unifying themes of guiding beliefs and the cultural risk matrix, you can stop and start your reading at any point.

Ordering Information:	Ballinger Publishing Company 54 Church Street Cambridge, Massachusetts 02138
Call:	(617) 492-0670
Specify:	ISBN 0-88410-997-6
Price:	$16.95

The Corporate Steeplechase: Predictable Crises in a Business Career

Srully Blotnick

Facts On File

© 1984
283 pages

Evaluation: A serious and engrossing analysis of the crises people are likely to encounter in the various stages of a business career. Blotnick reports the findings of his long, ongoing research study with a good mixture of case histories and pertinent commentary.

Thesis: It is possible to identify, anticipate, and overcome the obstacles many of us put in the way of attaining fulfilling careers in business.

Audience: For anyone at any stage of a business career; even if you are completely satisfied with your present position, you are likely to learn something of potential value to yourself, your peers, or your subordinates.

Reading Time: 7 to 9 hours.

Author

Srully Blotnick, a psychologist, heads his own research and consulting firm. He also writes a regular column for *Forbes*. Dr. Blotnick is the author of *Winning* (1979), *Getting Rich Your Own Way* (1980), and *Computers Made (Ridiculously) Easy* (1984)—all byproducts of the study on which this book is based.

Audience and Intentions

In the late 1950s, Dr. Blotnick and his team of researchers became convinced that "answers to a wide variety of questions about people and professions could be determined through a study of work-related hopes versus realities as the years went by." They put together a population sample of approximately 5,000 individuals: 2,000 active in a career; 1,500 of their children over the age of 13; and 1,500 unrelated university students.

From 1959 to the present, these people have been interviewed regularly about their achievements and frustrations at work. The researchers expected to "see what serious problems people could reasonably expect to encounter, decade by decade, in the course of a business career." Their definition of "business" covers a wide variety of professional activities, including "the large majority of civilian occupations in the United States." They studied not only corporate managers, but physicians, scientists, lawyers, architects, and many others.

Blotnick and his colleagues found that most people create their own difficult situations at work. Nonetheless, Blotnick contends that "it is possible to anticipate and overcome the hurdles that have brought many a budding career to a dead halt." People erect these "hurdles" themselves by failing to perceive the shifts in both their own personalities and the demands of their jobs. As a result, they continue to use inappropriate tactics. But because these crises are "largely predictable" and shared by many others, it is possible for alert business professionals to "foresee and prevail over the most important obstacles they will encounter."

By identifying the hurdles or crises most common to professionals in their twenties, thirties, forties, and fifties, Blotnick hopes to help readers at any stage of a business career to recognize, avoid, and overcome these obstacles to career fulfillment.

Summary

Chapter 1: Introduction (10 pages)

For centuries we have believed that most people have one true profession that perfectly fits their personalities and their needs. It should follow, then, that anyone who is sufficiently self-aware can select the right vocation, given correct information. Since the 1950s, social scientists have been attempting to teach people about themselves and the professions in order to make the "perfect" match. But people continue to change as they mature, and professions evolve as well, although not in the same direction or rate as the people who practice them. Indeed, the jobs actually change the people who work at them. Initial expectations also play a role: people educated in the liberal arts and sciences are particularly susceptible to career crises because they often enter the pragmatic world of business through a combination of choice and circumstance. The result of this mixture of expectations and evolutions is a tangle of maladjustments and frustrations. In **The Corporate Steeplechase**, Blotnick attempts to identify patterns in these tangles and thus to help people recognize and cope with crises in their careers.

Part I: The Twenties: The Theatrical Age

Chapter 2: Finding the Right Public Stance (15 pages)

People in their twenties use their personalities—their ability to be liked and to act out roles—to further career goals. They try on a wide range of "cloaks" in their early twenties; but those who are most likely to be successful choose a role that fits their personalities well and concentrate on it in their later twenties. Others continue to adopt whatever personality fits the situation, although they believe they are concentrating on job skills. These people are using a personality-oriented approach rather than a work-oriented approach to get ahead.

Typically, this latter group becomes devoted to self-promotion. Ultimately, given their hunger for instant acclaim, they never discover where their true talents lie. People who are gifted in one area but think their real strengths are in another straddle an abyss that can engulf them. Understanding one's strengths is critical on the job, even if some are rarely or never used.

Chapter 3: The First Career Crisis: No Career (15 pages)

A substantial proportion of children raised in middle and upper-middle-class families unwittingly spend their lives trying to be all things to all people. Subsequently, they are unable to make and stick to career decisions or develop a valuable specialty of their own. Work then becomes simply a way to make money. Instead of distributing their involvement between work and personal relationships, they concentrate solely on the personal. In time they begin to despise work and blame their jobs for their unhappiness. They focus their energy on "beating the system" by trying to do as little work as possible. They become increasingly disenchanted.

Unfortunately, many people exhibit this pattern of adjustment in their twenties. An excessively social orientation in high school and college tends to produce an excessively financial orientation on the job. In time, work is regarded only in terms of its monetary rewards, or lack of them.

Chapter 4: Beating the System (25 pages)

Many people can be expected to have difficulty making the transition from school to work. Former vocational students in such fields as accounting and education generally have an easier adjustment than students in academic fields such as history or English. Surprisingly, however, people who drop out of college because they couldn't "get into it" have trouble getting into work as well. Most become frustrated and obsessed with beating the system. Some people even develop conflicting allegiances to school and work and never find satisfaction in either arena.

When people who have gone to college because of its promise of financial rewards do not receive the kind of salaries they expected, they blame the system and begin to cheat at work. They not only withhold their best efforts, but they also refuse to expand their abilities. They harm their careers by avoiding risk and honest involvement.

Part II: The Thirties: Standing Out in a Crowd

Chapter 5: Is It Independence or Merely Insubordination?
(18 pages)

Business requires adherence to an unspoken code of conduct that is more restrictive than any most people have experienced since adolescence. Subordination is rewarded; insubordination is penalized. Some people respond to this discipline with an adolescent intensity that can harm their careers. They attempt to become distinctive by asserting themselves in a way that fails to harmonize with the group. This is a synthetic independence because it is simply a reaction against the expectations of others. Its costs include loss of goodwill and opportunities for promotions and increased responsibilities.

On the other hand, people with a strong and healthy sense of their own uniqueness are able to handle challenges to their independence at work. They are able to distinguish independence from individuality; they can be subordinate without loss of self.

Chapter 6: The Switch from Individual to Team Effort
(14 pages)

People in the business world promote the concept of teamwork, but rarely practice it. They are afraid that becoming part of a team will make them invisible and thus unlikely to receive either credit or promotions. They also believe that once they are in a team situation they will be unable to get out. The reality is just the reverse: well-functioning teams tend to be only temporary phenomena.

Despite America's preoccupation with spectator sports and the respect shown for teamwork, we tend to think of the team as a well-disciplined army with faceless individuals performing rote, robotlike tasks. The problem is exacerbated by some of the people who espouse teamwork in an attempt to suppress everyone but themselves.

Part III: Changing Jobs

Chapter 7: The Job-Change Checklist (18 pages)

In today's business environment, people change jobs frequently, and not all changes are due to poor adjustment. Highly motivated people tend to leap into new opportunities without stopping to consider the benefits as well as the frustrations of their current employment and without investigating the new situation. It is important for those contemplating a job change to assess the economic and financial health of the industry, the company, and the particular division that interest them. They should also investigate the power and indispensability of their potential supervisor, the number of people being hired for comparable positions at the same time, and the fallback positions available at nearby firms.

Chapter 8: A Mass of Expertise—Plugged into Nothing (18 pages)

While it is true that businesses take on the character of the people who work in them, the reverse is even more true: people are absorbed by their surroundings, especially in the eyes of the customers. This has special significance to people changing firms or leaving to start their own businesses. Even if the customers like them and have reservations about the firm, they will usually stick with the status quo rather than move with the individual. Subconsciously, customers view the migrating professional as an object of fear and uncertainty once divorced from his or her customary surroundings.

The trouble for the exiting employees and the expectant new employer is compounded when they deceive themselves about customer loyalty. It is hard not to take personally the tendency for clients to be lazy and stay put, but one must be realistic about one's ability to walk off with the firm's customers. Large companies in particular are surprisingly adept at holding onto their clientele.

Chapter 9: Easing the Transition (13 pages)

When people change jobs, the old business does not come to a halt; new people are assigned to the vacated position. This is especially true in larger firms, where certain employees may be indispensable but not irreplaceable. When departing workers realize this truth, they can be hurt emotionally—as well as financially. Their replacements will have greater success in retaining old customers, because the customers are lazy, the old firm is familiar, and the old firm must actively pursue them to stay in business.

The outcome of a job change can be improved significantly by preparing customers for the coming event as soon as possible. If customers can be made to see the change as an increase in prestige for the person making it, they are likely to consider this sufficient reason to make the shift to the new firm themselves.

Part IV: The Forties: Anxiety about Becoming Obsolete

Chapter 10: Becoming Indispensable to the Firm (13 pages)

Contrary to popular belief, even among professionals, the forties are the most dangerous years for people in business. Despite years of accomplishment, workers in this decade of life develop anxieties about their worth to the firm; they cease to advance; they lose their momentum.

Managers in this age group have typically reached a plateau in the corporate hierarchy and no longer have a large professional peer group by which to gauge their success. They have become valued specialists in the organization without realizing the extent of their independent authority. They become defensive of their territory and destroy their relationships with younger, up-and-coming subordinates.

Chapter 11: Pressure from Above and Below (12 pages)

People in their forties worry consciously and subconsciously about becoming obsolete at work; they are afraid of being thrust aside by those who are better informed. Such fears would be treated as a challenge in more energetic years, but they are a real threat to those in this decade who have lost their direction. Their first response is to obstruct the ideas of more alert juniors—until they are perceived as boulders in the path of progress. They then become intermediaries for the younger people to the top, passing on every suggestion as though they were simply conduits rather than decision makers. In time, top management realizes that the active talent is at the lower level and perceives the executive in his or her forties as "dead wood."

Chapter 12: Staying in the Mainstream (12 pages)

Statistically speaking, people between the ages of 37 and 53 receive fewer work-related compliments; often they hear nothing. For some reason we assume that this age group is so secure and task-motivated that they don't need recognition or praise. Unfortunately this is not true, and the consequences of "unappreciated" executives seeking approval from subordinates and superiors instead of new achievements can be severe both for these people and for their companies.

One of the alarm bells of this condition is the aforementioned obsolescence anxiety. When it sounds, the appropriate response is *not* a search for gratification by the victim or synthetic stroking by top management. Instead, afflicted executives must recognize that they will get little approval and direct their energies to perfecting their job specialties. They must become self-starters again.

Part V: The Fifties: The Problem of No Heirs

Chapter 13: Manipulating the Boss (19 pages)

Executives in their fifties feel a need to guide the next generation, to pass on what they have learned from years of experience. Consequently, they often unwittingly "adopt" a subordinate and attempt to develop a relationship that will also advance that person's career. The process is sometimes thwarted, however, by money and loyalty. Senior executives fear that the youngsters they have tutored will leave the firm and make good financial use of their advice elsewhere. For their part, juniors are more interested in "mentors" as agents of assistance to their careers rather than as dispensers of wisdom.

As a result, few of these relationships work out well for both sides. The elders' emotional needs mesh with the juniors' ambitions, but what ensues is usually manipulation of the senior executive. Backing away and doing nothing, which is the usual response, will not fulfill the pressing desires of managers in their fifties. Something else is required.

Chapter 14: Choosing the Right Heir
(9 pages)

Impediments to close relations across the generations at work are institutional rather than psychological. Top management can take the lead by *slowly* making the necessary changes; the process should not be hurried because it takes time to master. They should treat the "adoption" as a business investment and select the appropriate subordinate. The right candidate is likely to be over 40, competent, relatively quiet, and respected by the senior executive. The elder managers should be choosing students, not personable sidekicks. They should also not worry about defections to other firms, because there are compensations: The process of teaching is too valuable to be lost, and good teachers also learn from their students.

Part VI: High Achievers

Chapter 14: The Hidden Pitfalls of Self-Employment
(21 pages)

The single greatest reason for failure among the self-employed is a lack of self-discipline. They are unable to focus on and develop a specialized skill or area of expertise that can be exploited as a competitive advantage. Instead, many lose direction and become generalists; excited by new fields, they let customers dictate their activities and, by trying to do all things for all prospective clients, do nothing with the kind of distinction that will be recognized in their local business community. They become remarkably like people in their twenties: their chief virtue is flexibility.

The self-employed can take several steps to monitor their propensity to deviate from their strengths. They can, for instance, keep track of how much time they spend alone and thus eager for any contact. They can also note how tired they feel after a project, knowing that excursions into unfamiliar areas create nervous exhaustion. What is often called "burnout" should really be termed "juggler's strain in the haphazardly self-employed." Some versatility should be sacrificed for more productive long-term career goals.

Chapter 16: People Who Have Succeeded and Don't Know It (14 pages)

Several people in the midst of outstanding careers remain oblivious to their accomplishments. They have trained themselves not to celebrate the successful conclusions of projects as a device to continue to motivate themselves to do more. They downplay what they have achieved in the past to heighten the importance of the present and future. While the process works, it extorts an enormous price because it bankrupts people on a daily basis. Every day they start with no past triumphs, and they are driven to succeed. They are caught in a trap of rising expectations of their own making: whatever they do now, they will have to exceed tomorrow.

It is thus the dedicated workers who create crises for themselves. They can, however, help themselves as well by learning to stop throwing away past achievements. If they allow themselves to enjoy what they have accomplished by savoring the completion of a project, they can release excess pressure and thus promote more efficiency for future operations. Moments of self-congratulation can be brief and private and still produce results.

Postscript (6 pages)

People erect different hurdles for themselves during the different decades of their careers. In their twenties, people damage their professional prospects by unknowingly acting out roles that are incompatible with their true personalities. In their thirties, they develop distorted notions of teamwork that critically limit their ability to work with others effectively. While many workers in these years worry about keeping up and getting ahead, the burdens fall most heavily on those in their forties. People of this age must be concerned with loss of career direction and deteriorating relationships with peers and subordinates. Managers in their fifties and sixties allow themselves to develop destructive attitudes toward younger employees and thereby lose a chance to satisfy emotional needs. In all ages, recognizing the predictable crises can help the alert professional avoid or overcome these threats to career success.

The Corporate Steeplechase has a very sparse index, no bibliography, and only about a dozen footnotes. Its source is Blotnick's 25-year ongoing study. The four-page "Appendix on Methodology" supplies the technical description of the study and includes a few references.

Evaluation

Presentation

The Corporate Steeplechase provides a useful combination of the general and the specific. Fairly long narrative case histories are interspersed with succinct commentary. The stories of individuals are effectively presented and carefully selected to reveal the characteristics of the age group they represent. There are no composite figures. The author's conclusions are explicit and to the point, with no wasted motion. Most chapters provide summaries of the main points. The postscript to the book restates the thesis and reviews the crises experienced in each decade.

The writing is matter-of-fact and professional; the presentation is consistently even. The tone is knowledgeable and self-confident without approaching arrogance. The author has his opinions well in hand and does not hesitate to dismiss popular notions as "rubbish" or "drivel." Yet this is not dry material. There are very few statistical tables; the evidence is almost all anecdotal. You will find yourself getting interested in the case histories and caught up in the problems of the ages. The author also spices his exposition with a little wry humor. It all makes for stimulating reading.

Content

The back cover of the book jacket quotes William Simon as saying, "After a flood of 'how to' career books, it's refreshing to read one that asks 'how come?'" We agree with this insight. **The Corporate Steeplechase** is not a "how to" book at all, but a compilation of thoughtfully presented analyses of the nature of work and business in America. It is a serious and at times even philosophical work, the product of a lifelong research study.

Blotnick's approach is descriptive rather than prescriptive. He reports in careful detail what he and his colleagues have discovered about the hurdles we create for ourselves in our professional careers, but he is parsimonious with his advice on how to deal with them. He clearly assumes that an alert and self-aware reader will be able to recognize impending crises on the basis of the descriptions he provides and deal with them as the individual situation demands. This is not a "pop psychology" book; it does not give pat answers to everyone's troubles.

In addition to the personal benefits **The Corporate Steeplechase** is able to provide, it should also prove to be a valuable management tool. It identifies reasons for many puzzling behaviors and work attitudes that we may be called upon to identify in our peers and subordinates as well as in ourselves.

Reading Suggestions

The Corporate Steeplechase promises only information and insight, not a ready path to success. In that regard, one should not rely on it for easy answers, but rather for a penetrating analysis of problems common to business professionals. We recommend reading the entire book, not just the chapters on your own age group. Break your reading at the ends of major parts, because the case histories tie together the chapters dealing with the different decades. This is especially true for chapters 10–12 on crises for people in their forties.

The introduction will tell you all you need to know about the study population and the issues addressed. The appendix is for academics or professionals concerned with technical questions. Be sure to read the postscript; it reviews the major points thoroughly and succinctly.

Ordering Information:	Facts On File, Inc. 460 Park Avenue South New York, New York 10016
Call:	(212) 683-2244
Specify:	ISBN 0-87196-840-1
Price:	$17.95

Disconnecting Parties: Managing the Bell System Break-Up: An Inside View

W. Brooke Tunstall

McGraw-Hill

© 1985
226 pages

Evaluation: An informed account of the planning and implementation of the AT&T divestiture during 1982–83 that also communicates the emotional intensity of the participants. The author, an insider with considerable responsibility, draws some lessons for managing a complex change.

Thesis: The AT&T break-up is not only a dramatic corporate story with significant lessons for managers and public policymakers; it is an important human and cultural story as well.

Audience: People who were part of the Bell break-up; managers, consultants, and academics not involved but interested; the concerned general public.

Reading Time: 5 to 7 hours.

Author

W. Brooke Tunstall was corporate vice president of organization and management systems for AT&T and director of divestiture planning. He is now a private management consultant.

Audience and Intentions

Tunstall has clearly defined ambitions for his book. He intends to tell a corporate story, a human story, and a history. In telling the corporate story, he hopes to capture "the drama of the government's divestiture order, the managerial challenges to AT&T and its responses, and the lessons that managers and students of business might glean from the experience." In more mundane terms, he wishes to relate "how the divestiture was accomplished" by describing the decision-making process and the implementation plans.

The human story tells how "a family of one million employees ...turned the extraordinary spirit that had built and sustained the Bell System to the awesome job of dismantling it." Finally, **Disconnecting Parties** is meant as "an account of how a historic corporate culture, shaped to function by one set of rules, turned to face a future in which not only its business environment but also all of the rules would change."

Tunstall warns that his work "represents a singular perspective" from the "central staff vantage point" he occupied during the divestiture. The story was, he says, "too epic, too turbulent, too multidimensional" to be rendered in its entirety. Because of the "substantial potential for bias and oversight," the author cautions, the book should be read as "a narrative of events and opinions from one manager's perspective, not as an official AT&T account."

Tunstall goes on to identify three groups of intended readers. First, "it is for those who were part of the action—so that they might see more clearly...how their involvement fit into the larger tapestry of events." Second, it is for the professional managers, consultants, and academics who wish to understand more about the divestiture and gain insights "useful in conducting their own affairs." Finally, **Disconnecting Parties** is addressed to a general audience "eager to share an insider's view not only of what happened but also of what it all means."

Summary

Chapter 1: The Historical Context: AT&T under Siege (18 pages)

For the better part of a century the Bell System's unique position was that of a private enterprise with a public trust, made possible by regulation substituting for competition and the corporate goals of universal availability and superior quality. The extraordinarily successful phone system was challenged by explosive technological change that offered policymakers new alternatives and choices for the future.

The recent regulatory record was also a series of competitive challenges that elicited incremental deregulatory actions by the FCC. By the end of the 1970s large sectors of the telecommunications market were fully competitive, or nearly so. At the same time, Congress was demonstrating no inclination to counter the FCC's drift, and the Justice Department was suing AT&T for monopolization of trade.

That case was settled on January 8, 1982, with the agreement known as the "Modification of Final Judgment" (MFJ). AT&T agreed to divest to free itself from further litigation and the hopeless situation of "regulated competition." The corporation also wished to comply with, rather than buck, the flow of public desires.

Chapter 2: Divestiture Planning Diary (71 pages)

The planning and implementation of divestiture proceeded through the eight quarters of 1982 and 1983.

First Quarter, 1982. The top executives of AT&T began the active management of divestiture by identifying six major questions that had to be answered. This framework was animated by the managerial philosophy to balance the interests of constituents—shareholders, customers, employees, and the public—in all decision making. The presidents of the Bell Operating Companies (BOCs) formed six study groups to address the central issues and turn philosophy into action. On his own initiative, a middle manager polled hundreds of experts to draw up a comprehensive set of divestiture assumptions. These were used as a script to establish schedules and objectives for individual departments.

Second Quarter, 1982. Chairman Brown directed his staff to develop planning guidelines to comply with the MFJ. The core of the process was the Directors Planning Group (DPG), composed of key middle managers. The DPG worked around the clock seven days a week and consulted nearly everyone in composing the huge guides to be used by the BOCs.

Third Quarter, 1982. Thousands of people in all parts of AT&T and its subsidiaries came together in committees and task forces to execute the plans formulated in the first two quarters. This ad hoc network grew spontaneously and included heavy input from the BOCs. The Restructure Implementation Board (RIB) became the superordinate administrative agency to focus everyone's efforts and settle disputes. RIB tracked progress out of two "war rooms" in central headquarters.

Fourth Quarter, 1982. The responsibility for planning and implementing was AT&T's; the MFJ provided only very broad guidelines and gave the right of approval to Judge Green's court. Chairman Brown decided on January 1, 1984, as the date for divestiture and targeted November 30, 1982, for submission of the Plan of Reorganization (POR), which was to be a complete and legal document. Thus lawyers had to be brought in to work with managers and technical experts to develop the POR. Feedback on a preliminary draft identified 15 core issues to the BOCs. Most of these were settled in the fall president's meeting, which included the designated CEOs of the new regional companies. Remaining issues were handled by the Justice Department and Judge Green.

First Quarter, 1983. The shift from planning to implementation necessitated a new set of guidelines for the BOCs, Long Lines, and Western Electric that spelled out thousands of activities, assumptions, responsibilities, and timeframes. The effort had moved to the front lines. At the same time, however, senior management began an assessment program to identify problem areas that needed special attention.

Second Quarter, 1983. Assessment was carried out by a series of detailed questionnaires and region-by-region meetings between AT&T, BOC, and Western Electric officers, focusing always on making the 1/1/84 deadline. The assessment could not still everyone's apprehension, but it did red flag three trouble spots: access service, contracts, and billing systems. In addition to addressing these concerns at the BOC presidents' conference, top management made a plea for collective leadership and set a new, internal target date (October 1, 1983) for divestiture.

Third Quarter, 1983. Bell's strength, its high integration, proved an Achilles' heel threatening divestiture. People and assets had to be apportioned fairly, new companies created, cultures modified, and scores of computer programs and data bases sundered.

The dress rehearsal of what was called "functional divestiture"—he October 1, 1983, internal deadline—proved useful in identifying operational difficulties: 3 of 11 areas were still in a condition dangerous to success. Strains were evident between AT&T and the BOCs—and with employees, who struck for 15 days.

Fourth Quarter, 1983. The October 1st report to the presidents' conference was in two parts: (1) a complete and final assessment on the status of divestment and (2) a projection of the likely experience customers would have in the future. The first noted that 4 of 11 major areas were in good condition, 6 showed cause for concern, and 1 (access service) was in serious condition—an overall evaluation of "concern." More disturbing was the portrayal in part two of frustrated and confused customers no longer able to meet their communications needs with one-stop shopping.

By now the public had become interested in the ramifications of the break-up. Most business professionals thought divestiture was a bad idea, but Wall Street bid up the price of stock in the new AT&T.

Chapter 3: Restructuring—"Balkanizing Bell" (52 pages)

The MFJ required that the 22 BOCs be spun off from AT&T, but gave management the freedom to reorganize the divested companies any way it saw fit and to form a central services staff for them. Consequently, the one nation that was the Bell System was Balkanized into nine different states: seven regionals replacing the BOCs, a central staff, and AT&T.

Reorganizing the parent company was the most radical transformation. It involved separation of 75 percent of the assets to the seven regionals, absorption of 136,000 employees, redesign of systems, documentation, stock transfers, allocation of resources, and division of the network eight ways. The task was complicated by regulatory constraints, new freedoms to compete, loss of established contracts, and a search for a new mission. AT&T went through a functional realignment that included reducing the general staff from 13,000 to 2,000 by dispersing employees to other units.

AT&T Communications and AT&T Technologies were created as the two main subdivisions of the "new" AT&T. The first was the integrating unit, consisting of the network, marketing, external affairs, finance, personnel, and legal affairs. The second unit was organized to take advantage of market opportunities. It included Bell Labs, network services, technology systems, AT&T International, consumer products, and information systems.

Launching the seven new regional companies was far more complex than regrouping the 22 BOCs. Each new CEO had to develop new missions, goals, strategies, and structures for his independent business. Their unique leadership skills plus the differing economic, regulatory, and financial environments gave the regionals distinctive characters in a very short order.

The central staff for the regional companies came to be called Bell Communications Research. It grew, almost reluctantly, out of a systematic search for those activities that had to be done centrally. Eventually an 8,800-person service organization was created that was heavily weighted toward meeting technical needs. Some analysts believe it could be a prototype for other industries seeking legally to coordinate competition.

Chapter 4: Cultural Transformation (17 pages)

Perhaps AT&T's most difficult task was managing the psychological divestiture: redefining the corporate culture to bring the value system into congruence with the new competitive mission. At the precise moment of AT&T's major transition, the telecommunications industry was becoming competitively volatile, adding to the turmoil and dislocation. Some aspects of the company's strong and long-entrenched culture, such as the service ethic, could be retained; others would have to be adapted.

Even before divestiture, Bell management embarked on a slow, consistent, and conscious cultural change. They began shifting the corporate mindset to a competitive orientation, rewarding and recognizing entrepreneurial managers. Leadership came from Chairman Brown and retiring AT&T President Ellinghaus. The latter's study found a corporate identity crisis after divestiture; people believed the company had lost its mission and they had lost their roles. They did, however, retain a faith in AT&T and pride in themselves as companion feelings to their outrage. Brown responded with a redefinition of values indicating that top management had turned in a positive direction. Only time will tell if the whole corporate body can take on a new orientation.

Chapter 5: Lessons Learned: Managing the Transition

(11 pages)

The divestiture management approach was remarkably effective. It was accomplished in minimal time, with the least possible impact upon the corporation's constituencies and with no major disruption in the nation's telephone service. Given that AT&T's experience was exceptional, it still offers lessons for companies facing complex adaptations in a changing business environment, lessons that validate traditional management theory.

(1) In times of rapid change, you can't wait for all issues to be clarified; you must mobilize early, trust your instincts, and start with your best-guess assumptions. (2) Delegate responsibility by pushing down implementation (not policy) decisions and providing maximum leeway for independent thinkers and technical experts. (3) Set overall guidelines at the top and escalate stalemated issues. (4) Communicate what is known and what is still unknown widely and often. (5) Set firm target dates to challenge, not intimidate. (6) Send a top-down message of confidence that you can believe in and that will communicate new values.

Chapter 6: Lessons Learned: Managing Before and After (14 pages)

Contrary to accepted belief, managing in a competitive environment may not be harder than managing in a highly regulated one. It is, however, unquestionably different. AT&T had to forge a new mission and a new decision-making infrastructure. Each of nine strategic components had to be entirely reformulated into a completely new, coherent system.

The changes were (1) general strategic orientation driven by market opportunities rather than technological considerations; (2) a top-down planning process instead of a bottom-up; (3) financial policies predisposed toward growth, not dividends; (4) technology development emphasis on application more than basic research; (5) pricing policies formulated on costs, with no subsidization of local service; (6) market strategy focused on customized rather than standardized offerings; (7) product strategy geared to short rather than long life cycles; (8) organizational orientation decentralized along product/market lines instead of centralized and structured by functions; and (9) corporate culture risk rather than consensus oriented.

Chapter 7: Crucial Questions for the Future (8 pages)

Several questions deserve inquiry in future years. (1) What were the moving forces behind the break-up of the Bell System? Specifically, what roles were played by the Justice Department, the Congress, the courts, and technological developments? (2) What government procedure best serves the public interest? Was a courtroom trial the best way to formulate national telecommunications policy? (3) Did AT&T take too long to accept a changed public mandate? Could it have held out longer?

The author believes that a speeded-up regulatory process or new legislation could have better served the public interest. He feels that more far-sighted public policymaking could have avoided the loss to the nation occasioned by a dismantled integrated network.

Chapter 8: A Final Reflection (4 pages)

One of the most striking lessons of divestiture may be that ostentatious displays of enthusiasm that sometimes pass for commitment are less important than authentic trust between managers and employees. Bell people managed the divestiture because of a long tradition of trust and because they had the technical skills, capacity for team-work, and discipline to do the job.

* * *

Following chapter 8 is an epilogue consisting of eight cartoons from newspapers and magazines, representing the "lighter side of divestiture," and an appendix with the complete text of the "Modification of Final Judgment."

The book does not have footnotes or a bibliography. Publication data is provided in the text for sources mentioned or quoted. Most of the sources are AT&T publications. There is also a detailed index.

Evaluation

Presentation

Tunstall's narrative moves smoothly and coherently. He gives us a sense of what the AT&T divestiture must have been like for the people involved, even though the author doesn't relate any personal or company anecdotes. His purpose is served well by the copious figures, tables, quotations, and boxed lists that help clarify a complex situation. **Disconnecting Parties** is a good technical presentation.

Yet, those considerations aside, it is important to realize that the book is a *dramatic* account. For all its professional competence, **Disconnecting Parties** frequently communicates a high emotional intensity. AT&T is seen as fighting what amounts to a military action—against an obsessed Justice Department and a biased judge, supported by a confused Congress and an indifferent (until too late) public.

Although the war theme is deliberate and military metaphors consciously employed (and commented upon by the author), it is not done to manipulate the reader to support the author's point of view. The tone instead is an essential expression of the mood that prevailed during (and after) divestiture and as such is an important element in the dramatic/historical presentation. This is, after all, intended to be a human story.

It is, in addition, an insider's view, although not a personal story. Tunstall may not hide his feelings, but he does limit exposure of his role in the proceedings and clearly labels his opinions. This is AT&T's story, told by a very involved and interested observer/participant.

Content

Disconnecting Parties consists of the history of AT&T divestiture planning and implementation during 1982–83 and the lessons thereof. The history encompasses chapters 1–3. Chapters 4–8 contain the lessons. They spell out with extraordinary precision what the Bell story can teach us about managing change in general and managing a transition from a regulated to a competitive environment in particular. They also articulate basic questions about public policymaking and express a strong opinion concerning the value of trust between managers and employees.

In evaluating this extremely rich mix, we cannot lose sight of the book's two distinctive presentational qualities: (1) the insider's view and (2) the intense emotional tone running through the structure of the story. The first warns us—as the author himself does—that what we gain in increased proximity to the action we lose in objective detachment. Nonetheless, we feel that we can trust the accounts of the proceedings, certainly not discount the motivations ascribed to Bell personnel, and respect the careful consideration given by the author to the management lessons to be learned.

The emotional intensity that Tunstall can subdue but not extinguish is of value because it communicates so well the scope of the story in a way that objective description could not. **Disconnecting**

Parties is a drama: it expresses the pain and the pride of the people directly involved in the divestiture. This is a rare business book that engages our feelings as well as our intellect.

Reading Suggestions

How you respond to the book will depend upon your involvement with, and opinion of AT&T. Those detached from, or even hostile to, the now-fragmented giant should keep in mind the last point made in the Evaluation that opinions and emotions expressed by an insider are revealing in and of themselves. A more restrained objectivity would not tell us as much. Those in Tunstall's primary audience who were "part of the action" may be in for an emotional as well as educational experience.

Readers wishing additional perspective on AT&T and the break-up are directed to *Disconnecting Bell* (reviewed in **BBR** volume 2, number 5) and *Heritage and Destiny* (volume 1, number 1).

Ordering Information:	McGraw-Hill Book Company 1221 Avenue of the Americas New York, New York 10020
Call:	(212) 512-2000
Specify:	ISBN 0-07-065434-4
Price:	$17.95

The Winning Streak: On Sustaining Success When Times Are Tough: Lessons from Britain's Top Companies

Walter Goldsmith and David Clutterbuck

Random House

© 1984,* 1985
204 pages

Evaluation: A well-organized and carefully structured examination of the characteristics that distinguish successful British companies. The book is less ambitious and less intense than its American model, *In Search of Excellence*. It is of interest to a U.S. audience because it demonstrates how principles of good management can be effective in mature industries operating under very tough environmental conditions.

Thesis: It is possible to identify eight characteristics that successful companies have in common and that unsuccessful firms seem to lack. In addition to those qualities, well-managed firms are adaptable to cultural change and committed to winning.

Audience: Primarily for practicing managers; also for academics, interest groups such as union leaders and public officials, and the concerned general public.

Reading Time: 5 to 6 hours.

*Originally published in Great Britain in 1984.

Authors

Walter Goldsmith is chairman and chief executive of Korn Ferry International Ltd. and chairman of Leisure Development Ltd. He is a Fellow of the Institute of Chartered Accountants.

David Clutterbuck is the editor of a number of business publications and a correspondent for *The Times* and the *Observer*. He is the author of *How to Be a Good Corporate Citizen*.

Audience and Intentions

Goldsmith and Clutterbuck have set out to create a British *In Search of Excellence*—taking account, they say, "of the very different industrial circumstances, practices, and legislative environment in Britain." They have identified several companies that have prospered during the recent economic turmoil and sought reasons for these successes.

The companies, often in mature and declining industries, met three criteria for selection: (1) a high growth in assets and profit over the last decade, (2) a consistent reputation in their industry as a leader, and (3) a solid public perception as a good company.

The authors carried out an extensive set of interviews with top management and a wide range of employees of 23 firms meeting these criteria. Further, they obtained documents and responses to questionnaires from 15 additional firms that satisfied at least two of the three standards. To round out the study—and as a validity check—they also examined companies that failed in order to determine whether their newly identified elements of success were lacking in those cases.

Goldsmith and Clutterbuck's purposes in organizing their findings into a book are to "attempt to isolate the characteristics of good management," to explore the attitudes and behavior of managers and employees of successful firms, and to "establish a set of standards" by which these companies judge themselves and "against which other enterprises can be judged."

The authors consider **The Winning Streak** to be directed expressly at three audiences. First, for the practicing manager they hope to provide "help in the establishment of a practical framework for the improvement of his own company." Second, for the academic they want to offer "a starting point for more intensive analyses of key issues." Finally, for a more general audience—including union leaders and government officials—they expect "to give a better understanding of how successful companies work."

Summary

Chapter 1: Winning as a Matter of Style (7 pages)

Although each company in the study might emphasize different elements, they all exemplified eight common characteristics. (1) They demonstrated strong *leadership*: visible top management, clear objectives, and a vision of the future. (2) They created *autonomy* by encouraging entrepreneurial spirit. (3) They maintained tight *controls* on areas that mattered, through consensus rather than formal rules. (4) They generated commitment and *involvement* by managers and employees. (5) They had a strong *market orientation*. (6) They practiced *zero basing* (keeping in close touch with the fundamentals of the business). (7) They lowered internal barriers to change to stimulate *innovation*. (8) They built *integrity* into their way of doing business.

Chapter 2: Leadership (16 pages)

The first of three elements of good leadership is the visibility of the leader. Top managers in these successful companies are always out in the field visiting operations and listening to the troops on the front line. When employees have a positive view of top management—that is, trust and not necessarily liking—their motivation is higher.

Second, leaders provide a clear sense of mission in which they believe passionately and in which they are able to inspire others to believe. They develop broad statements of purpose that show staff at all levels where the company wants to be.

Finally, leadership entails identifying clear objectives for the company and freeing the resources so that people can pursue them. Top management thereby creates an environment where middle and junior managers can be leaders as well.

Chapter 3: Autonomy (18 pages)

Successful companies in the study have the maximum of autonomy, except in certain key areas of such importance that centralized controls are necessary. For decentralized firms, several common factors are evident. First, they have small headquarters and bureaucracies and relatively few levels between the chairman and the operating unit heads.

Second, they maintain the business as much as possible in small units, each with its own clear mission tied into overall organizational goals. Third, these independent units have informal systems of cooperation, and, fourth, have action-oriented, informal management teams.

Autonomous organizations attract ambitious, motivated people; increase productivity; instill enthusiasm; and create a positive attitude toward risk taking.

Chapter 4: Control (12 pages)

Firms in the study keep central controls to the minimum compatible with the fulfillment of their objectives. The fewer the controls, however, the more strictly line managers are expected to adhere to them. What they choose to control depends on the structure of the industry and the company culture. Most have tight rein on capital expenditure. But in all cases, the controls are simple and the reasons for having them are obvious.

Other elements common to the successful companies studied include: (1) tight controls on finance to ensure that the money goes where it will be most effective, (2) constant feedback of results from decentralized units to headquarters, (3) close attention to business planning, and (4) high standards of quality coupled with high expectations for people to conform to them.

Chapter 5: Involvement (29 pages)

Successful companies extract an uncommon amount of personal commitment, dedicated hard work, and involvement from employees. These firms have both a strong productivity orientation and a strong profit orientation. Employees identify with overall company goals and share company values. They have what could be described as "pride in ownership," identifying themselves as much with the company as with their occupation or skill. This sense of pride is engendered through profit sharing, broadening of people's exposure to the business, and promoting employee participation in decision making.

Also important is a high degree of communication in which top management passes down information and listens to people below, both through mass gatherings and face-to-face encounters. Good companies also pay well to attract the best people and emphasize monetary incentives. They promote from within and train their people for growth. Finally, they recognize the social side of work—the enjoyment factor—and treat each individual with genuine respect. They use paternalism to create a good working environment.

Chapter 6: Market Orientation (11 pages)

For these companies good customer relations and a thorough understanding of their markets are essential. They are also the routine of daily business. This market orientation is expressed in terms of (1) extensive efforts to maintain the strength of the company brands, (2) swift and comprehensive dealings with complaints, (3) emphasis on quality control, (4) a healthy interest in market information, and (5) a practical market focus in research and development programs.

Chapter 7: Zero Basing (7 pages)

Successful companies are almost fanatical about keeping contact with the fundamentals of their businesses; they monitor and reassess their activities against a few core principles. In the same way that they must balance autonomy and control, so too must they resolve the conflict between the need to innovate and the need to stick to fundamentals. Companies in the study accomplish this balancing act by paying close attention to details. They thus manage to avoid making serious mistakes and to catch and correct those they do commit.

Chapter 8: Innovation (17 pages)

Good companies are open to new ideas. They value innovations that advance the corporate mission. They see innovation as a competitive tool that can be applied to such areas as marketing and finance as well as technology development.

Innovation is fostered by removing barriers to change. This task is accomplished with a clear framework of objectives, constant feedback and information from management, growth opportunities, an organization structured for innovation, and incentives for taking acceptable risks.

Innovative firms also have a natural curiosity about how things are done elsewhere, an international perspective, and R&D directed toward defined market needs. The chief executive plays a role, too, in focusing attention on innovation.

Chapter 9: Integrity (8 pages)

Chief executives of the companies studied embrace integrity with a passion. They are convinced their business can not operate without absolute honesty. They see it as a positive attitude toward "doing the right thing" in all relationships with customers, suppliers, employees, and the public at large. In a business sense this means always working to generate long-term relationships with these constituent groups based on trust and loyalty. As a result, these groups (particularly suppliers and employees) treat the company in the same manner in which it acts.

Chapter 10: The Family/Founder Influence (7 pages)

Leadership style and company culture are heavily influenced by the character and reputation of the founder or recent family chairman. The influence of the family or founder seems to consist of four elements. (1) They provide continuity. (2) They offer a long-term perspective and commitment. (3) They present the opportunity for the wider values of paternalism. (4) They can more easily establish a public identity that reinforces a brand image. Successful family companies are also able to avoid the disaster of incompetent family members ascending to positions of power. Such firms tend to demand a great deal of family recruits.

Chapter 11: Success versus Failure (24 pages)

An ancillary investigation of *un*successful firms reveals that they demonstrate a lack of some or most of the characteristics common to companies in the main study.

Ineffective leadership is a crucial factor in many company failures. Top management is not visible and is unable to define either objectives or a vision of the future. A thorough executive house cleaning is frequently necessary for a turnaround.

Unsuccessful companies are characterized by an extensive bureaucracy and centralized operations. Trust is minimal and delegation difficult. Controls are improperly applied; data are imprecisely focused. A long-term perspective is lacking, as are high standards for products and employee/manager behavior.

Unsuccessful companies fail to instill pride in ownership because they are slow in adopting employee share programs and are incompetent in eliciting employee participation. They are low payers and do not understand the motivating potential of incentives. They tend to promote people who will freeze the company culture. Training may be ineffective because it is not focused on clearly defined company objectives.

Unsuccessful companies lack an understanding of their markets; they fail to maintain their brand names. Such companies have trouble enforcing quality control and handling customer complaints. They lack the discipline to attend to details. Innovation is thwarted by the "not invented here" syndrome. They may have integrity, but they fail to get the message across to customers and employees.

Conclusion (4 pages)

This investigation suggests a few important questions for further consideration. The first question is whether corporate culture can be changed. Evidence from the successful companies indicates that they were able to adapt behavior to stimulate cultural change. Second, does the shape and composition of the board influence success? Research is negligible, but anecdotal reports favor the inclusion of activist, non-executive directors. Finally, still to be determined is the importance of a winning attitude. Again, indications from executive comments are that an overwhelming commitment to winning is perhaps the single characteristic most likely to be found in every successful company.

Appendix 1: The Winning Streak in Smaller Companies (18 pages)

Peter J.A. Herbert, a member of the staff of the Henley Management College, examines whether the traits of success found by Goldsmith and Clutterbuck in larger companies can also be observed in smaller firms. He considers each of the eight elements in turn and concludes that they are present, with the differences one would expect under different operating conditions.

Appendix 2: Three Statements of Company Philosophy (7 pages)

The authors reproduce statements from three of the companies studied: Standard Telephones and Cables (STC), H.P. Bulmer Holdings Limited, and Saatchi & Saatchi.

Appendix 3: The Questionnaire (7 pages)

The authors identified 34 characteristics of company style: 8 from *In Search of Excellence* and 26 from interviews with the 23 successful companies. They asked the chairmen of another 15 firms that didn't quite meet the three criteria for success to rank their companies according to these characteristics. The results are presented here in tabular form.

* * *

The book concludes with a one-page bibliography of additional sources and an index.

Evaluation

Presentation

This is a very well-organized book in which structure dominates without becoming mechanical. Chapter 1 defines the eight characteristics of business success as observed in Britain; chapters 2–9 elaborate on those characteristics. Chapter 10 addresses the special topic of founder/family influence. Chapter 11 examines unsuccessful companies on the basis of the eight characteristics (and many subcharacteristics)—which makes for a good review of the major points of the book. Chapter 12 introduces three additional considerations that apparently did not have sufficient anecdotal or documentary support to join the core eight. Finally, if chapter 11 is a mirror image of the structure of chapters 1–9, appendix 1 puts them in miniature for smaller companies (appropriately, in smaller print).

Symmetrical structure pervades the chapters themselves. The core chapters all begin with definitions of characteristics and a list of common elements, which are developed in the main sections, and must conclude with a "summary" that focuses on the larger picture rather than relisting attributes.

Each of the characteristics and subcharacteristics is illustrated with several short examples from the subject firms. These appear to be carefully chosen to support the framework and not for their entertainment value. The stories are clearly presented and certainly to the point, but few are memorable.

The book is, in short, very British: well crafted, correct, understated, and reserved. British spelling, punctuation, and vocabulary should not distract or disturb anybody. The examples may not be as interesting in themselves as inside information because the companies are not, for the most part, familiar to American readers. From another perspective, however, they command our attention precisely because they are *not* American. We learn, for instance, about a British CEO who "mucked in" (helped out) in a pinch by making tea for the over-busy workers. On only one occasion was a passage unclear because we didn't recognize a brand name. Also, some typically British expressions such as "the shoemaker sticking to his last" may require the aid of a dictionary. (In this case, sticking to the last means sticking to the business one is best at, as the shoemaker sticks to his "last," or shoe form.)

The authors provide some guidance to the world of British commerce by listing the major executives by company name in the front of the book and describing the business of those companies in reasonable detail. They write well and efficiently. The prose lacks the intensity we have come to expect from many major American business books, but it makes for surprisingly pleasant reading.

Content

An important part of **The Winning Streak** for most American readers will be Tom Peters's preface, in which he compares Goldsmith and Clutterbuck's conclusions with those of *In Search of Excellence*. Most of the characteristics of success are, of course, the same. Peters does, however, note three differences: (1) the emphasis on leadership (which is the focus of *Passion for Excellence**), (2) the element of control (which Peters says he was correctly criticized for omitting), and (3) the stress on integrity.

We agree with Peters's further assertion that **Winning's** treatment of unsuccessful companies (chapter 11) adds considerably to the study. Also of merit is his opinion that the book is valuable because it shows how unglamorous, mature industries can succeed

*Reviewed in *BBR* volume 3, no. 4; also reprinted in this volume.

in a very difficult business environment. It ought, as he suggests, give heart to a few U.S. firms in such cities as Detroit and Pittsburgh.

Goldsmith and Clutterbuck's work is also very close to the two *Excellence* books in another very critical aspect: methodology. **Winning** comes to its conclusions on the basis of informal (and some formal) anecdotal evidence, that is, stories from managers and brief, possibly superficial, case histories. Readers must also be aware of the book's criteria for "success": reputation and growth over the last decade. Those are not necessarily poor standards, but they do suggest—as the authors themselves point out—that "success" can be fleeting.

In other words, when you put great stock in learning the lessons of the winners, you had best be sure of how "winning" is defined and be ready to reexamine your premises if and when the winners begin to lose. Peters and Waterman have had to dodge a few bricks on these issues as well.

Finally, we need to consider why there is relatively so little passion in this British search for excellence. Possibly, as we suggested earlier, it is simply the British style to be more reserved. Whether or not this lack of intensity—or conviction—is related to national character, **Winning's** goals are nonetheless, far less ambitious than those of the *Excellence* books.

Goldsmith and Clutterbuck are not signing up for Peters's "revolution" with this volume. More modestly they set out to (1) provide a practical framework for managers, (2) identify key issues for research by academics, and (3) offer insights into successful companies for the general public and interested parties—all of which they accomplish.

The authors are very honest about the limitations of their information and the scope of their recommendations. Nor is this academic false modesty; the book's examples lack detail and depth (and passion)—perhaps because of the authors' limited experience. It may be that if they follow Peters's path after *Search* and gather more data and more enthusiasm, we will see *Winning with a Passion*, a sequel in which the "revolution" will be joined. Until then, there are still a few things we might learn from our British cousins in this carefully constructed book.

Reading Suggestions

Be sure to read both Peters's preface and the authors' introduction. Take a few minutes as well to skim over the descriptions of the companies and people who are the subjects of the study; they will not often be identified in the text. If you are interested in small businesses, look through appendix 1. Chapter 1 and the conclusion will serve as an adequate executive summary—as will this review—after your first complete reading of the book.

Ordering Information: Random House
201 East 50th Street
New York, New York 10022

Call: (800) 638-6460

Specify: ISBN 0-394-54485-4

Price: $19.95

The New Competition: What Theory Z Didn't Tell You About Marketing

Philip Kotler, Liam Fahey, and Somkid Jatusripitak

Prentice-Hall

© 1985
292 pages

Evaluation: A professionally presented book with excellent blending of concepts and case histories that adds significantly to the literature analyzing the Japanese model of success by (1) emphasizing and detailing Japanese market strategies, (2) identifying the general source and direction of further Asian competition, and (3) outlining appropriate responses of U.S. firms.

Thesis: The "New Competition" is made up of Japan and several developing nations in Asia; it is characterized by the now commonly recognized elements plus one neglected factor: excellence in strategic marketing; to meet this challenge, U.S. firms must understand the "New Competition" and create effective strategic marketing responses.

Audience: Business leaders who must compete with Japan and other talented Asian marketers; people concerned with the U.S. economic future.

Reading Time: 7 to 9 hours.

Authors

Philip Kotler is the Herald T. Martin Professor of Marketing at the Kellogg Graduate School of Management of Northwestern University. Dr. Kotler is an internationally respected consultant and lecturer on marketing. His classic text, *Marketing Management*, has been translated into several languages, including Japanese.

Liam Fahey is a consultant and a teacher at Boston University. He is founder and editor of a monthly publication on strategic planning. Somkid Jatusripitak is an authority on the Far East. He recently completed his doctoral program at Northwestern.

Audience and Intentions

The authors began their investigations into Japanese marketing strategies after observing that the books explaining that nation's astounding economic success neglected the marketing factor. They consider this oversight significant because not only is the "deep Japanese penetration into world markets not over," but other Asian nations—South Korea, Taiwan, Hong Kong, Singapore—are applying Japanese tactics to win "sizable shares of key global markets." The world may, in fact, soon be in the "Pacific Century."

Kotler and colleagues categorize the West's current responses to just the Japanese challenge as "still superficial and inadequate." Serious study and action will thus be required to meet what they term the "New Competition" from several developing nations in Asia. The "New Competition" is characterized by

1. A disciplined and skilled workforce
2. Cooperative labor-management relations
3. A competitive medium- and high-tech orientation
4. Acceptance of a lower rate of return over a longer-term horizon
5. Government assistance for business
6. Protected home markets
7. A sophisticated business and marketing strategy

The purpose of the book is to examine the "New Competition," particularly as exemplified by Japan. It briefly documents the first six factors listed above before concentrating at length and in detail on the neglected seventh element: "the range of marketing strategies used by the Japanese to identify opportunities, enter markets, penetrate them deeply, confront opponents, and maintain dominance." Finally, **The New Competition** offers recommendations on how Western firms can best respond to this marketing challenge.

The book is thus both concept and action oriented. As such, it is directed specifically toward business leaders who must compete with the Japanese and other emerging Asian economic forces and less pointedly toward others concerned with global business strategies.

Summary

Part I: The Marketing Battleground

Chapter 1: World Class Marketeers: The Japanese (19 pages)

In 1945 the Japanese economic, political, and social fabric had been destroyed; Japan lacked natural resources and had no understanding of Western markets; its products were considered to be of poor quality. The Japanese miracle is that it overcame all those handicaps, and the miracle is not yet over.

In addition, the developing nations of Korea, Taiwan, Singapore, and Hong Kong are applying and adapting Japanese methods to provide more serious competition to Western firms. By the 1990s, India, Indonesia, Thailand, Malaysia, and the Philippines will be added to the list of new competitors. By the next century, 25 percent of the world GNP will be generated in the Pacific Basin.

The Japanese are currently making strong inroads into such industries as computers, construction, chemicals, pharmaceuticals, and machine tools. Japanese firms are increasing their investments in other countries as well. The challenge can be met only by complete analysis of their methods, neglecting no important factors.

Chapter 2: The New Competition's Success Formula
(17 pages)

The Japanese success is the product of a complex interplay of several important factors, classified into four environments: sociocultural, government-business, competitive, and organizational. The additional factor of their marketing strategy orientation has made Japanese firms dominant in several important world markets.

The sociocultural environment includes such cultural characteristics as a strong sense of group responsibility and a willingness to work hard toward long-term goals. The competitive educational system is also important. The government-business environment was reformed by the American postwar occupation. The Ministry of International Trade and Industry (MITI) came to play a major role in guiding and supporting business, as do the general trading companies. In the competitive environment, the intense domestic competition has allowed Japanese firms to test different production and marketing strategies. The organizational environment is also justly renowned for the contributions of lifetime employment, employee training, consensual management, and labor-management cooperation. The final essential link has been the Japanese marketing strategy.

Chapter 3: The Market-Takeover Process: How the West Was Won (20 pages)

The role of marketing functions on two levels: (1) government selection of target industries and (2) individual firm design of effective strategies. The national government aided the domestic auto industry, for instance, by adopting protectionist measures and by formulating policies to stimulate exports.

On the micro level, Toyota (the most successful Japanese auto company) created a four-step marketing strategy for the U.S. market. Stage 1 entailed identifying opportunities as guided by the concepts of market segmentation and cross-cultural analysis. Stage 2 involved developing market-entry strategies: build a smaller, improved car; pursue penetration pricing; begin in the West Coast and "roll out" eastward; and advertise heavily in target markets. Stage 3 required implementing market takeover strategies; refine the product to meet consumer demand; price lower than other makers; improve dealership quality; and advertise heavily but cautiously. Finally, Toyota moved to stage 4, market-share maintenance. The company continued to monitor changing consumer tastes and continued to learn and improve. It is representative of other Japanese firms in that it knows marketing is more than just selling.

Part II: Far Eastern Marketing Strategies: The Road to Domination

Chapter 4: Identifying Opportunities: Knowing Where to Strike (25 pages)

Successful Japanese companies practice formal long-run strategic planning and marketing implementation. The first step in this process is identifying and managing market opportunities.

At the macro level, Japan as a nation identifies target industries for special treatment. Government agencies, especially MITI, make the selections and devise support measures. MITI is also instrumental in channeling funds to target industries, controlling foreign investment, and managing turbulence.

Individual Japanese firms must also exercise their own initiatives. They have tended to follow five strategic approaches. (1) Search out opportunities "provided" by U.S. business when it ignores or poorly serves certain market segments. (2) Create opportunities through research and technical development. (The 1970s and 1980s have seen a transition from "provided" to "created" opportunities.) (3) Find opportunities through product and market creativity. (4) Adapt to changing customer preferences. (5) Learn from competitors by studying their weaknesses and limitations. All these activities require extensive information collection, analysis, and dissemination.

Chapter 5: Entry Strategies: Carving the Niche (18 pages)

Successful Japanese companies devote a lot of time to market feasibility studies and marketing research prior to entering a market. They will design a plan that integrates all the marketing elements and that links price, quality, and service.

Japanese firms have emphasized three categories of products for their foreign market entries: (1) lower-cost products, (2) products with innovative features, and (3) high-quality products. They follow a market-share pricing strategy that sets a low entry price to build up market share and establish a long-run position. In distribution, they have chosen whatever means had the best chance of gaining market access. Usually that meant offering higher than normal commissions and focusing on a specific distributor system or geographic area before rolling out nationally. The Japanese also tend to support their products with heavy advertising.

Chapter 6: Penetration Strategies: Broadening the Base (19 pages)

The effective integration of product development strategies and market development strategies makes the Japanese formidable competitors. They manage their product development by product line stretching, product proliferation, and product improvement to broaden the base of market support. These modifications are made in conjunction with market segmentation and sequencing. Flexibility is the key: the Japanese adapt their marketing mix to prevailing competitive conditions.

The Japanese "learn by doing"; they are always alert to market reaction. This incremental thrust allows them to adapt to external conditions. Product developments and improvements make little sense unless targeted at clear customer segments. In this regard, Japanese firms seem to be more market- and customer-driven than product- and technology-driven.

Chapter 7: Confrontation Strategies: Battling Competition on All Fronts (28 pages)

There are five types of strategies that firms may adopt as they enter and try to penetrate a given market. These are flanking, frontal, encirclement, bypass, and guerrilla.

The flanking strategy engages competitors in the product-market area where they are weak and the attaching firm is strong.

Its goal is to gain a position from which to launch a major assault at a later date. It is a niching strategy that works best in an expanding industry with distinctive market segments.

The frontal attack becomes necessary when new firms have advanced sufficiently to confront the dominant firms. Limited frontal attacks based on price or R&D advantages are more likely to succeed. Frontal attacks are very risky and so should only be considered when a firm has sufficient resources and a sustainable competitive advantage.

An encirclement strategy consists of producing more types and styles of products at both higher and lower price ranges or expanding to fill adjacent market segments. It forces competitors to protect all sides at once. The strategy requires an extended period of resource commitment.

The bypass strategy avoids competition by developing new products, diversifying into unrelated products, or diversifying into new geographical markets. The risk entails going beyond the firm's area of expertise.

The guerrilla strategy is designed to harass and demoralize in order to secure eventual concessions. It works best for smaller firms building toward a broader competitive challenge.

Chapter 8: Maintenance Strategies: Defending Market Leadership (22 pages)

Challenges to Japanese dominance include (1) anti-Japanese sentiment in several developed countries, (2) counterresponses by the United States and Europe, (3) competition from other Asian nations, and (4) changes within Japan itself.

To maintain its leadership, Japan is likely to adopt one or a combination of defensive strategies: position defense, mobile defense, preemptive defense, counteroffensive defense, flank-position defense, and strategic withdrawal.

The first, the position defense, is a fortlike response that is risky and unlikely to appeal to a nation enamored of constant product/market development. Japan thus prefers to adopt a mobile defense through market broadening and market diversification. It practices the preemptive defense by building on current product-market strengths. The counteroffensive defense consists of counterattacking the aggressor. The flank-position defense discourages attack by fortifying flanks—in business terms, by increasing productivity. Finally, the strategic withdrawal narrows the scope of one's position by abandoning a product or market.

Chapter 9: Building a Global Position (24 pages)

Even small and medium-sized Japanese firms have learned to view the entire world as a potential market. Global marketing has benefited the Japanese in three ways: (1) the experience curve effect and economies of scale keep prices competitive, (2) a decentralized production system holds down costs, and (3) the ability to transfer profits from successful markets to smaller fledgling markets finances inroads into new markets.

Japanese firms have followed one of three global expansion paths. The first begins with building a domestic market as home base, then using developing countries as springboards from which to enter the U.S. and European markets. This approach was used with cars and watches. The second path also begins with Japanese domestic markets but then goes to developed countries before expanding into developing areas. Option 2 was used with computers. Finally, the Japanese have followed the developed countries—home market–developing countries route for products (such as videotape recorders) that the domestic market was not yet ready to support.

Chapter 10: Linking Strategy, Organization, and Decision Making (18 pages)

Japanese patterns of strategy thinking, organization design, and decision making have contributed greatly to Japan's competitive success in global markets. Their strategic mentality consists of (1) a long-term focus, (2) a competitive as well as customer orientation that seeks to defeat competitors, and (3) a definition of success in terms of product and market development. The important macro-organizational structures are the business groups such as the Zaibatsu and the general trading companies. On the micro level, Japanese firms do not commit themselves to a hierarchical structure. Their decision making reflects a blending of bottom-up and top-down processes, multiple perspectives, and a thirst for information.

The implications of the Japanese patterns are that competing companies need to develop a strategic mentality, or even a strategic culture. The culture must permeate the entire organization. Thus it will need constant reinforcement over an extended time period.

Part III: Meeting the New Competition

Chapter 11: Responding to the New Competition (27 pages)

The United States has four potential strategic responses to the challenge of the "New Competition." It can respond competitively in the public arena with such tactics as tariffs and quotas or cooperatively with reduced trade barriers. The private sector can also respond cooperatively or competitively. Joint ventures, licensing agreements, and mergers are examples of the cooperative approach; improving quality and service and lowering prices are variations of the competitive.

U.S. firms can strengthen their ability to compete by (1) measuring their comparative advantage, (2) monitoring the factors affecting that advantage, (3) understanding the Japanese success model, (4) considering the whole range of strategic options, (5) planning for the long run, and (6) developing more competitive strategies. The best sequence of strategies will depend on the size and positioning of the individual firm. Studying the steps taken by Motorola, Xerox, and IBM will provide some ideas.

Chapter 12: Toward Strategic Marketing in the Twenty-First Century (19 pages)

There are three closely interrelated elements of strategy development: (1) understanding strategy, (2) creating and sustaining a strategic organization, and (3) managing strategy analysis.

Strategy is a process of making choices; its goal is to create and sustain competitive advantage. Strategic choices are constrained by market factors and the firm's goals. Customers are more important than competitors in determining strategy. Commitment, flexibility, and creativity are the keys to a successful strategy.

The organization's structure needs to coevolve with its strategy. Strategic leaders form strategy circles and create a strategic culture. They focus on basic insights, not numbers, in strategic analysis. They identify and manage the major issues. They learn through action.

Appendix: How Did the Japanese Learn Their Marketing?
(5 pages)

Marketing was invented in Japan around 1650 when the Mitsui family created the first department store. Western influences on marketing were not significant until the 1930s. Marketing became more important in Japan in the 1950s as a consumer goods society began to develop. Most theory came from U.S. books and teachers, notably *Marketing Management* (Kotler) and Dr. Edward Deming. Since the 1960s, Japanese firms have become more market oriented; their style reflects the interplay between Eastern and Western thinking and experiences.

* * *

There is an extensive section of annotated source notes and occasional brief comments following the appendix. The notes are organized by chapter and page number but not numbered. This format is inconvenient to use, but the main text is not cluttered with numbers or footnotes. The book has an index but no bibliography.

Evaluation

Presentation

Kotler and associates present their ideas in what should be standard professional and academic style. There is a very effective combination of the general and the specific, of the conceptual and the concrete. The explanations of the principles are clearly and logically written, aided by a great many well-conceived diagrams.

The authors give us a host of details and pertinent examples with several fairly long case histories.

Authorial personalities do not intrude into the work. Although Kotler and colleagues offer a number of important recommendations for U.S. firms wishing to compete in the world marketplace, they support the validity of their advice and the urgency of its application on the basis of well-constructed and thoroughly documented arguments rather than their own authority.

A few relatively minor flaws detract a bit from this very readable book. There are, for instance, far too many lecture-style announcements of what is to come next in the chapter ("Now we will do X and then Y. . . ."). **The New Competition** is also somewhat repetitious, mostly in its examples. Occasionally terms are defined late in the book after they have been used several times earlier (e.g., "dumping"). For the most part, however, the material is well organized and efficiently presented.

Content

It is important to be clear about what **The New Competition** has to offer. Certainly its greatest achievement is to go beyond the established literature in defining the factors that have generated Japan's economic "miracle." The authors review the by-now-familiar elements and add one that seems to have eluded other analysts: sophisticated marketing strategies. The authors' conviction that Japanese marketing skills are critical to their success is buttressed by a detailed and comprehensive examination of the whole Japanese strategic approach. It adds significantly to our understanding.

The second contribution of the book is the definition of what it calls the "New Competition." Although concentration on Japan's past triumphs makes this sound a great deal like the "old" Japanese competition that has terrorized U.S. business for the last two decades, there is a "new" character of sorts. The book identifies several emerging Asian economic powers with which the West must contend *and* stresses that—in contrast to many commentators who believe the Japanese have lost momentum—Japanese firms will be challenging world markets in new areas and defending their dominance in many of the old. The battle, it seems, has only just been joined.

Finally, **The New Competition** describes the nature of the responses U.S. firms might make to contend with the emerging power of the Pacific Basin nations. The book provides reasonably detailed strategies, considering the range of the industries and companies involved. The strategic framework and the scope of possible marketing approaches is potentially very valuable.

This work is, consequently, more than another "secrets of the Japanese" book. Kotler and his associates have added a significant factor to the equation for business success in the world market and offered U.S. interests guidance in solving that equation to their own advantage.

Reading Suggestions

The good mixture of concepts and case histories and the illuminating diagrams make this a fairly easy book to read and understand. The natural breaks in your reading sessions will come at the major divisions. If too much time passes between your reading of part II on the Japanese marketing strategies and part III on possible U.S. responses, take a few minutes to review the key points in chapters 5–8 so that the terminology will be familiar.

Ordering Information: Prentice-Hall, Inc.
Englewood Cliffs, New Jersey 07632

Call: (201) 592-2000

Specify: ISBN 0-13-612078-4

Price: $19.95

Beyond the Quick Fix: Managing Five Tracks to Organizational Success

Ralph H. Kilmann

Jossey-Bass

© 1984
300 pages

Evaluation: A book that offers a very professional presentation of a complex, three-dimensional model of the business world and a systematic program for achieving high performance and good morale over an extended period of time.

Thesis: Organizational success requires a view of the world as a "complex hologram" with complex problems, a response with an integrated five-track program that is implemented in sequence, and a commitment by top management.

Audience: Managers at all levels, though particularly top management; consultants; researchers.

Reading Time: 7 to 9 hours.

Author

Ralph H. Kilmann is professor of business administration and director of the Program in Corporate Culture of the Graduate

School of Business at the University of Pittsburgh. He is also president of Organizational Design Consultants, Inc., a management consulting firm. Dr. Kilmann's academic training is in management and industrial administration.

Audience and Intentions

Kilmann has observed that every few years a new organizational approach appears to offer simple answers to everyone's managerial problems. Recently the concept of corporate culture has been in vogue. Usually these single-answer approaches are discarded in favor of the next new all-purpose solution. Each proves ineffective, not because it is inherently flawed, but because it is applied incorrectly in isolation as a quick fix. The fault, Kilmann believes, lies in our devotion to the myth of simplicity. He insists that we must, therefore, develop *and implement* complete, integrated programs appropriate to a highly complicated environment.

Beyond the Quick Fix is intended to provide such a program for creating and maintaining organizational success. By "success" the author means "achieving both high performance and high morale over an extended period of time...by managing *all* controllable variables in the organization." His "complete program" consists of five "tracks": culture, management skills, team building, strategy-structure, and reward system.

Kilmann asserts adamantly that these five tracks must be integrated and implemented in sequence to be effective over the long haul. "Each track," he says, "sets the stage for the next." Further, "if any of these tracks is implemented without the others, any effort at improving performance and morale will be severely hampered. Any benefits derived in the short term may soon disappear." The final element in Kilmann's thesis is the essential understanding and commitment of top management: executives must see their companies as complex, three-dimensional organizations and take responsibility for change.

Beyond the Quick Fix is directed at three groups of readers. The author wants it to show managers "how an orchestrated approach to organizational success can be undertaken" and how "to identify barriers" so they may be transformed "into channels for success." Because consultants play a vital role in this complete program, the book is designed to "expand their range of skills and methods" beyond their "pet" specialties. Finally, Kilmann hopes his work "will motivate researchers to develop other integrated programs for managing real-world problems."

Summary

Chapter 1: Principles for Organizational Success (29 pages)

Organizational success is largely determined by how well internal adjustments are made to the increasing "dynamic complexity" of the external world. In some cases what brought the organization success in the past will be destructive in the present. Managers tempted to "erroneously extrapolate" past false assumptions into the new reality will hurt their companies, which is why lessons from "excellent" companies may have only historical interest.

Both managers and consultants are also tempted to adopt the single approach that promises a quick fix or immediate success. There are, however, six key principles that explain why an integrated program is necessary and why a quick fix will inevitably fail: (1) The world should be viewed as a "complex hologram" (three-dimensional picture) rather than a simple machine; (2) resulting problems are complex rather than simple; (3) multiple rather than single tracks are necessary to solve these problems; (4) participative, instead of top-down, approaches to management are needed to capture all the expertise and information multiple tracks require; (5) managers may need to utilize internal or external consultants to conduct the very sensitive portions of the tracks; and (6) integrated approaches cannot be learned by quick reading—they must be studied.

Chapter 2: Theory Behind the Five Tracks (28 pages)

The theory that supports an integrated approach states that changes in several interrelated variables are necessary to achieve the intended results. The approach of this book is based on a theory that can be represented by the barriers-to-success model (see figure). Several of the barriers can be controlled by management through the five tracks and leverage points corresponding to the tracks: (1) culture, (2) managerial skills, (3) team problem solving, (4) strategic choices and structural arrangements, and (5) the reward system. Properly managed, these barriers then become channels to success. The uncontrollable barriers include the setting in which the organization exists, the human psyche, and the unstated beliefs or assumptions behind decisions and actions. These barriers can at least be monitored.

The five broad categories of an open system are the setting, organization, manager, group, and results. The single arrows show the primary impact one category has on another, culminating in a determination of decisions, actions, morale, and performance. The diamond in the center contains those "holographic aspects"—culture, assumptions, and psyche—that add the third dimension of depth to the model. The double arrows signify the strong reciprocal influence between the three below-the-surface aspects and the other categories. The model captures the multiplicity of angles of a complex, holographic view of the world.

Figure 1. Barriers to Success.

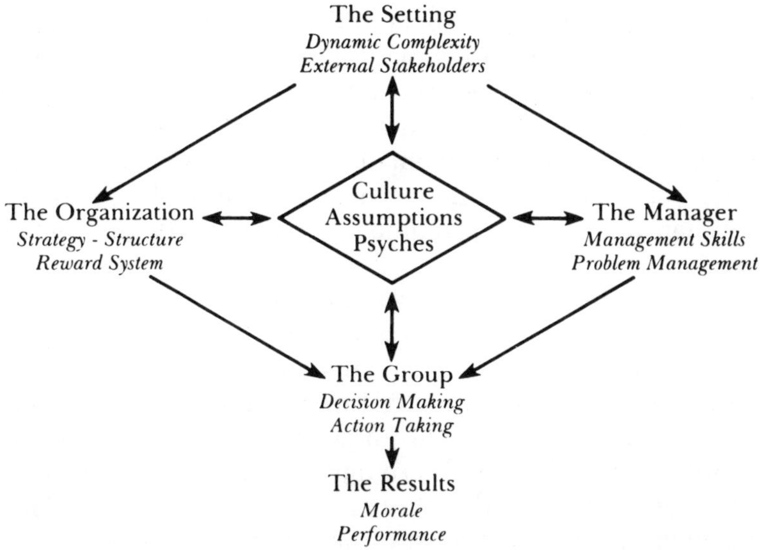

Chapter 3: Practice Behind the Five Tracks (32 pages)

Theory is useless without practice. The theory behind the five tracks pinpoints the barriers that block performance and morale; the practice behind the five tracks specifies how all individual barriers can be transformed into channels for success. The practice must be guided by a carefully constructed program for planned change. The planned change program for the five tracks approach is instituted in five stages.

The first stage is the initiation of the program, which occurs when the organization realizes that its old ways of addressing problems are no longer effective. The second stage is the diagnosis of the organization's problems. Ideally, independent consultants take charge here. The third stage is the scheduling of the five tracks; the fourth is their implementation. Finally, the fifth stage is the evaluation of the program's results. Additional activities may be necessary for one or more tracks, and the cycle of planned change continues.

Chapter 4: The Culture Track (34 pages)

Culture provides meaning, direction, and mobilization; it is the social energy that moves the corporation into action. In some corporations, however, the energy is diffuse; in others, it moves members in the wrong direction. "Culture shock" occurs when an organization suddenly finds that it has lost touch with its mission. Cultures become dysfunctional when left to themselves. Management that falls into this problem of cultural stasis continues to see and act out what made the organization successful in the past rather than adapt to the dynamic complexity of the present and future.

Culture can be controlled by managing the company's group norms. Assessing and changing cultural norms is a five-step process; it requires both consultants and managers to work to generate trust and commitment. First, all group members must list the actual norms that currently guide their behaviors and attitudes; most of these will turn out to be negative. Second, the group articulates new directions for the organization. Third, group members develop a list of new norms for organizational success. Fourth, they identify the "culture-gaps" between the actual and desired norms. And, fifth, they close those gaps. Members have to agree that the new norms will indeed be established and make provisions for group monitoring and enforcement. The older culture will reappear, however, unless the other four tracks are implemented in their turn.

Chapter 5: The Management Skills Track (36 pages)

The particular mix of skills required for successful performance depends upon the level of management: at the bottom, technical skills predominate; at the top, administrative, analytical, and conceptual skills are the most important. All skills must, however, be developed specifically to handle dynamic complexity, which requires that managers first sense and define problems before they select and implement solutions. Managers must also be able to distinguish between simple and complex problems.

Complex problems require the Hegelian inquiry system found in assumptional analysis. This method focuses on the underlying assumptions of an argument. Most individuals, for instance, do not question the hidden assumption that things will automatically be the same in the future as they are in the present. Assumptional analysis consists of six steps: (1) forming initial conclusions, (2) grouping participants around conclusions, (3) having the groups analyze their assumptions in terms of their certainty and importance, (4) having the groups argue their critical (uncertain and important) assumptions with each other, (5) resolving and synthesizing assumptions with a series of new groups formed from cross-sections of the old, and (6) synthesizing conclusions.

Chapter 6: The Team-Building Track (32 pages)

Effective group efforts require a whole additional set of energies and skills. Troublemakers must be managed before groups can be developed into fully functioning teams, and each group must be functioning well before the more complicated intergroup problems can be tackled. Because of the sensitivity of the personality problems involved, outside consultants will be needed.

The individual counseling process for managing the troublemakers consists of four steps: (1) identifying the troublemakers, (2) conducting the first feedback session with individual troublemakers to identify disruptive behaviors that will no longer be tolerated, (3) conducting follow-up sessions, and (4) concluding the sessions when behaviors terminate or when members can handle disruptive actions themselves.

The five steps of team building are (1) meeting with the work group to build trust and collect data, (2) diagnosing group problems, (3) deriving solutions and developing action plans, (4) implementing the action plans, and (5) monitoring and evaluating the results. In complex organizations, interteam building is also necessary. The five steps here parallel those for team building, except now the consultants and managers must examine how individual teams work, or fail to work, together.

Chapter 7: The Strategy-Structure Track (36 pages)

Strategy sets the direction for the firm; structure coordinates human and technical resources to move the organization in the intended direction. Determining strategy requires assumptional analysis. Designing structure requires understanding the different "task flows" between and within the various subunits of an organization. When making strategic choices, (1) utilize wide-scale participation, (2) examine underlying assumptions, and (3) encourage a creative synthesis. Once the strategic choices have been made, organize the firm's resources to achieve its mission.

Organizing the structure entails coordinating objectives, tasks, and people for each subunit of the organization. In addition, three important interfaces are necessary: (1) strategic—defining purpose and mission, specifying objectives and tasks; (2) structural—designing subunits to minimize task flows across boundaries; (3) job—reallocating time of people on tasks for maximum efficiency. Restructuring in a complex organization can best be accomplished by a computer program, such as MAPS. Organizations can avoid restructuring at every environmental crisis by adopting a Problem Management Organization that links the established operational structure with a "collateral" structure designed to work on new complex problems.

Chapter 8: The Reward System (33 pages)

Reward systems should be designed to attract and retain able individuals and to motivate people to high levels of performance. Many reward systems fail in the latter purpose, with unfortunate consequences in a complex world that demands more than routine performance.

Designing a performance-based reward system—the best way to motivate intrinsically for morale and extrinsically for performance—is a complex undertaking. In general, organizations must recognize the importance and flexibility of pay, determine how best to measure performance objectively (outcomes of work) and subjectively (process of working), link pay directly to measures of performance, and involve all participants in the planning. Specifically, they should follow a seven-step process: (1) form a collateral structure to work on the system, (2) review the types of reward systems, (3) form groups around alternative systems, (4) have each perform an assumptional analysis, (5) design the detailed reward system, (6) implement the system, and (7) evaluate it.

To communicate expectations, evaluations, and rewards to employees, managers must establish periodic performance reviews and frequent counseling sessions. The former tells employees how they are doing; the latter helps them improve.

Chapter 9: Commitment to Organizational Success (14 pages)

While the five tracks form the basis for organizational effectiveness and efficiency, top managers must also commit the time, energy, and resources to identify the barriers and transform them into channels for success. Without this commitment all efforts toward the integrated program will be wasted. Many executives, however, have been socialized to avoid this enormous responsibility, which is why guaranteed quick-fix solutions are so popular. The solution is to share responsibility with a trusted but diverse inner circle. Such an inner circle provides the range of information and expertise needed to manage dynamic complexity and the emotional support required to take action under conditions of extreme uncertainty, imperfection, and complexity. Organizational success is possible if managers are willing to adopt a new way of managing the "holographic" (complex, three-dimensional) world around them.

* * *

Sources for the book are listed alphabetically in an extensive bibliography. Chapters are documented in the academic fashion by citing these bibliographic entries where appropriate in the text. There is also a large, detailed index.

Evaluation

Presentation

Kilmann's main themes are methodically interwoven throughout all nine chapters and restated in the conclusion sections of the first eight. There is an excellent mix of the concrete and the abstract, with extended illustrations from AT&T, General Motors, Digital Equipment Corporation, and Westinghouse's Synthetic Fuels Division (SFD). The SFD case history—relating a consulting project of the author's—runs through chapters 3–8 and also serves to unify the book.

The material is very carefully explained. Kilmann makes excellent use of diagrams and lists to clarify some fairly complicated ideas and procedures. He integrates several long quotations into the text—especially in the early chapters—and they seem uniformly appropriate. The tone is serious, but calm and very self-assured. Kilmann knows that he has the answers and is convinced that he can make them work for us.

Content

Kilmann's thesis can best be summarized by the six principles enumerated in chapter 1. To paraphrase, he presents a view of the world as a "complex hologram"—rather than the simple machine we act as if we believe it to be—that generates complex problems that must also be analyzed three-dimensionally. The only adequate response to these problems entails an integrated, five-track program, implemented sequentially. The approach requires study, participative management, and coordination of tasks between consultants and managers.

This concept of a complicated, organic business universe seems infinitely more valuable than a mechanistic one that supposedly can be mastered by one-minute managing and harking to anecdotes of excellence. As Kilmann asserts in the final chapter, however, it requires a manager of intelligence and character to understand fully the ramifications of dealing with interrelated subjective (and hence uncontrollable) and objective factors and to commit resources, time, and career to the task of implementing the complete, integrated program. Clearly though, executives with the right stuff are here offered an impressive system with which to manage their organizations.

Unlike other theories of organization and management, Kilmann's barriers-to-success model will not let you pick and choose individual components. He feels, perhaps rightly, that there is sufficient flexibility in his system as is. You must, therefore, buy the whole system, which includes putting it into practice in the precise, prescribed sequences. Consequently, the ultimate value of **Beyond the Quick Fix** is determined by how far beyond the quick perception of a "complex hologram" you wish to go. Actually to put it into operation, you must be willing to commit yourself and your company's resources, follow the broad outlines of the script, and work for an extended period of time (six months to two years) with outside consultants also committed to and experienced with the five tracks.

We can easily recommend that you invest the few hours to read Kilmann's book and consider its thesis. It is a serious and substantial piece of work. What you do with its insights depends on the health of your organization and other alternatives available to well-read executives of strong determination.

Reading Suggestions

The book is well written and moves at a good pace, but requires more than the usual concentration. Chapters 1–3 go together and should be read in one session, if possible. After that, break as your schedule and energy permit. Try not to spread out your reading too much. Kilmann advises us to study, not skim—and he is probably correct. With this review as a reading guide, however, you should be able to study fairly expeditiously.

Ordering Information:	Jossey-Bass, Inc. 433 California Street, Suite 1000 San Francisco, California 94104-2091
Call:	(415) 433-1767
Specify:	ISBN 0-87589-620-0
Price:	$19.95

Re-inventing the Corporation: Transforming Your Job and Your Company for the New Information Society

John Naisbitt and Patricia Aburdene

Warner Books

© 1985
308 pages

Evaluation: An entertaining and stimulating book that is not as flashy as *Megatrends* but offers a valuable perspective on the future of business and work as well as a number of practical ideas and options.

Thesis: The economic forces of keen global competition and a declining industrial base—reinforced by the coming labor shortages due to the baby bust, the whittling away of middle management, and the definition of human resources as a company's competitive edge—are converging with the people-oriented values of the baby boom generation to create new corporate models for the 1990s.

Audience: Managers with the authority and/or desire to adapt their organizations to succeed in the near future.

Reading Time: 7 to 8 hours.

Authors

John Naisbitt is the chairman of the Naisbitt Group, a company that tracks and publishes information on social, political, technological, and economic changes. Naisbitt is a lecturer and corporate adviser and the author of *Megatrends* (1982).*

Patricia Aburdene is a writer and lecturer specializing in business topics. She is president of Search for Common Ground, a national security think-tank. Aburdene was an anonymous collaborator on *Megatrends*.

Audience and Intentions

Re-inventing the Corporation began as the business chapter of a more cosmic book by Naisbitt and Aburdene on "re-inventing the world we live in." As the length of the treatment grew, it evolved into a stand-alone work, although it remained, for the authors, a statement of the essential economic underpinning for the re-invention of society.

The book's background reveals the scope of the authors' thinking and reminds us of the premise behind their analysis of work and business: the "megatrends" they have identified and continue to monitor. In fact, however, this book focuses mainly on practical and topical issues, as the authors examine what should be done and what is being done by corporations to adapt to the changing environment.

Specifically, **Re-inventing** is "about taking advantage of the unusual opportunity this decade brings to transform your job and your company for the new information society." The authors propose to accomplish this task by explaining how "corporate prototypes" are "re-inventing the corporate role in society" and recognizing "the connectedness between corporate life and the other aspects of people's lives—the family, health, education."

In the process, Naisbitt and Aburdene hope to help readers interact with the new social environment described in *Megatrends*. Their aim is "not just to inform, but to inspire . . . by putting forth a catalog of solutions . . . [that] will encourage you to keep experimenting until you find what works in your company."

*Reviewed in **BBR**, volume 1, issue 1.

The "you" in the preceding statement—the audience for the book—is never identified explicitly. By implication, **Re-inventing** is intended for people with some authority in their organizations. It might also "inspire" anyone with sufficient initiative to instigate change or to seek employment with a "corporation" more in tune with the looming future. "Corporation," incidentally, is defined loosely by the authors and also includes any public or nonprofit organizations in which people work together.

Summary

Introduction (7 pages)

The convergence of social values and economic necessity will drive American business into new corporate, social, and economic models for the 1990s. The forces for change include (1) the shift to an information society, (2) the coming employees' seller's market, (3) the whittling away of middle management, (4) the continuing entrepreneurial revolution, (5) the emergence of the new varied work force, (6) the continued increase in the number of working women, (7) the growing use of intuition and vision, (8) the inadequacies of the education system, (9) the rising importance of corporate health issues, (10) the values of baby boomers now in management.

Chapter 1: Re-inventing the Corporation (35 pages)

Now and into the 1990s, three powerful trends are changing the environment and compelling corporations to re-invent themselves. They are: (1) the shift from financial capital to human capital as the key strategic resource in the information society, to the extent that people are now considered the competitive edge on the path to profits; (2) the whittling away of middle management by upwards of 15 percent because of the rise in self-management and the increase in use of computers; and (3) the labor shortages and coming seller's market as the new economy creates millions of jobs and the number of people entering the workforce declines dramatically.

The first ingredient in re-inventing the corporation is a vision of how your company fits into the business environment. In order to create a vision that will motivate people, the corporate leader must draw on an intuitive mind. The second ingredient is "alignment": attracting people who can adopt the leader's vision and share responsibility for achieving it. Alignment is possible only by grounding lofty concepts in the company's day-to-day environment.

Vision cannot be realized in the old bureaucratic structure. Several alternatives that facilitate communication and replace the "us vs. them" mentality include: (1) the small team, (2) the cross-disciplinary team, (3) the "biological" organization, (4) the partnership option, (5) the fellowship option, (6) the lattice organization, (7) the team CEO, and (8) Americanized quality circles.

Chapter 2: Ten Considerations in Re-inventing the Corporation (34 pages)

The following ten factors should be kept in mind when considering career moves or company policies. (1) The companies that create the best environments for personal growth will attract the best people. They can nurture individual development by having experienced people working with younger talent, structuring jobs holistically, and organizing learning experiences. (2) The manager's new role will be to cultivate an environment for personal growth. Thus managers may need more retraining than workers.

(3) Compensation systems that reward performance, innovation, and loyalty are being offered to ordinary employees as well as executives, giving every contributor a sense of ownership. (4) At the same time, there is a shift from hired labor to contract labor—employee leasing to reduce paperwork.

(5) The top-down authoritarian management style is yielding to a networking support system. (6) Companies are reorganizing themselves into confederations of entrepreneurs. (7) Quality will become paramount. (8) Intuition is gaining new respectability, in part because there is too much data. (9) Large companies are adapting the values of small business. (10) Quality of life is becoming important in the corporation as well as in society as a whole.

Chapter 3: Re-inventing Work (40 pages)

For the first time there is a widespread expectation in America that work should be fulfilling and fun. This belief—strongest among the baby boom generation—is a natural outgrowth of the affluent society. Fortunately, it is suited to the needs of information work, for which people must be committed and self-supervised. People who are having fun at work are aligned with the company's goals. There is thus a growing new compatibility between the needs of people and the needs of corporations in the information society.

To take advantage of this convergence, the workplace must be reorganized away from the notion that everyone should be treated the same and toward individualized work contracts, which include financial incentives and opportunities for personal growth. Corporations and people should take part in life/work planning that helps the individual decide on a fundamental life goal and formulate a plan for achieving it.

More and more, flexible work scheduling will be a tool for both employees and corporations to get what they want. Flextime, permanent part-time jobs, job sharing, and flexible benefits will be common. These devices will also allow the older worker—who *will* be needed—to remain in, or get back into, the labor force.

The 1990s will also be the decade of the entrepreneur. In addition to the shift to an information society, other forces drive the entrepreneurial boom: (1) corporations can no longer provide the security they once did, (2) new markets and new business opportunities are available, and (3) venture capital is searching for investment possibilities. For these reasons, the family business is also gaining appeal. Corporations will have to contend with this competition for scarce labor resources.

Chapter 4: The Skills of the New Information Society (25 pages)

Unskilled people constitute the one threat to the prosperity of the information society and the successfully re-invented corporation. We must therefore re-invent the education system now geared to the characteristics of uniformity and centralized control that were appropriate to the old industrial society. Education today needs to stress TLC—learning how to *t*hink, *l*earn, and *c*reate—beyond the basic skills of reading, writing, and doing mathematics.

Bringing quality and accountability back into education means teaching students to think logically: namely, to make generalizations, draw inferences, order facts, distinguish fact from opinion. One established approach is to make writing instruction part of all subject matter classes. In a constantly changing environment, learning how to learn is essential. It is a skill that requires openness, curiosity, and humility, and one that facilitates adaptation to technological, social, and economic changes.

Creativity is the corporation's competitive edge, the special talent that discovers the right market niche. Creativity can be released through such learnable techniques as meditation, daydreaming, and brainstorming.

For TLC and other skills, lifetime learning will be required. The adult education boom will grow, and learning will increasingly be scheduled for the convenience of the student.

Chapter 5: Education and the Corporation (34 pages)

Today there is a profound mismatch between what the workplace needs and what the schools are providing. As the pool of entry-level workers shrinks, companies will have to face the prospect of hiring graduates who are even more poorly qualified. As a consequence, corporations have become the nation's leading education activists. They are also becoming so involved in training themselves as to constitute a separate and vast education system. Three-quarters of large U.S. corporations provide remedial education and teach basic skills.

All across America, businesspeople are teaching in local schools, contributing equipment, and becoming role models for students. Corporations are leading the fight against illiteracy and contributing billions of dollars to education. They are forming partnerships with specific institutions, as in the decentralized adopt-a-school program. Cooperative exchanges allow teachers to work summers in business and corporate engineers and scientists to teach in the schools at company expense.

On their own turf, companies are becoming more willing to invest in people and their skills through training and education. These programs have become so vast as to represent an alternative education system. Businesses too small to form their own "university" rely on the community colleges for their training needs. By contributing to their employees' education, companies of all sizes are enhancing the quality of life—one of the ten considerations for re-inventing the corporation.

Chapter 6: Health and the Corporation (24 pages)

Now that people have become a company's competitive edge, it is vital that the company's people be healthy. However, health care is already one of the highest costs of doing business. To solve this dilemma, companies are adopting a "high tech/high touch" approach. High tech means using information technology to audit medical bills; high touch involves stressing prevention and wellness to cut costs.

Until recently, there was little incentive for companies or their employees to fight the health care cost spiral. But the federal government took the lead in holding down costs by the limitations it put on Medicare payments.

Corporations can do their part by (1) auditing health costs, with the help of medical experts; (2) organizing a local coalition of corporate cost busters; (3) self-insuring the company; (4) investigating, or even creating, HMOs; (5) joining a preferred provider organization (PPO); (6) making use of freestanding emergency centers and ambulatory surgicenters; and (7) creating a smoke-free workplace.

Companies can become wellness workplaces with programs that offer guidance on fitness, stress management, health screening, weight control, and nutrition. Wellness programs are good business because they (1) communicate a concern for people, (2) cut costs, and (3) attract good workers.

Chapter 7: Women and the Corporation (24 pages)

In the new information economy women are earning respect and power and forcing companies to recognize their legitimate needs. Working women have already had an impact by increasing the corporation's interest in flexible scheduling, flexible benefit packages, and the value of intuition. They have not, on the other hand, been as successful in narrowing the wage gap with men. In the future seller's market for labor, however, companies will have to pay women what they are worth—and subsidize day care, as well.

We are moving toward the time when virtually all women will work at paying jobs. Today as many women in their twenties and thirties work as men of that age. Women's work patterns have changed in a generation. Combining careers and motherhood—for those women who choose motherhood—means selecting from a variety of work options: permanent part-time positions, flextime, job sharing, and so on.

These policies are of value to corporations because they allow them to retain, or gain, the services of competent employees—a rare enough commodity that will become even scarcer. In addition, programs such as subsidized day care increase the productivity and morale of workers while reducing absenteeism and turnover.

Equal pay for equal work has not helped the overall wage gap because men and women are segregated into sex-specific jobs. Consequently, for all its troubles, the concept of comparable worth may be an idea whose time is coming. Again, corporations may want to become comparable worth employers to attract the best women and the best (fair-minded) men.

Chapter 8: Re-inventing the Corporation in Japan (24 pages)

To one degree or another, the trends taking place in the United States are also having an impact in all industrialized nations. Even Japan is being forced to re-invent the corporation—in ways that may appear small to some in the West but are most extraordinary to the Japanese.

One force for change is the very large degree of mutual economic cooperation and development between the United States and Japan. In time, some people may come to speak of "U.S.A.–Japan, Inc."

Japanese business is experimenting a great deal with what they call inside-the-company ventures, what is known here as intrapreneuring. Further, the consensus-building decision-making apparatus is being streamlined and even eliminated in some places. The work week is being adapted or shortened, and such famous management characteristics as lifetime employment, seniority-based promotions, and company unions are facing serious re-examination. Japanese firms are even hiring more foreign employees.

Conclusion (6 pages)

The booming information economy and the baby bust will create a seller's market for labor that will have a significant impact on the corporation. Companies must offer incentives—often in the form of flexible work schedules—to attract capable women and retain older employees. Corporations must also recognize the interconnectedness of work, family, health, education, and community. That means involvement in education, life planning, and wellness; it means shared interests with workers and communities/schools; it means linking profits and people.

* * *

The authors document their work with 30 pages of source notes; they also mention a few key books in the body of the chapters. There is a good, detailed index.

Evaluation

Presentation

In their new work, Naisbitt and Aburdene maintain elements of the distinctive style of *Megatrends* as, at the same time, they adopt more of the characteristics of standard professional literature. *Megatrends* was based on the "content analysis" of many local newspapers—a methodology that apparently impressed Naisbitt's audience more than it did traditional economic and social forecasters. Judging by its documentation, **Re-inventing** is the product of sounder standard scholarship. The authors have not abandoned their distinctive approach, but they appear to have moved farther into the accepted professional mainstream. **Re-inventing** is fast- paced and economically written in declarative sentences and short paragraphs—punctuated in the Naisbitt-Aburdene fashion, with summarizing aphorisms in bold type set off from the main text. In this book, however, these declarations are fewer in number, less pretentious, and less metaphorical. The tone is more down-to-business, muting a bit the gee-whiz flavor of *Megatrends*. Indeed, a little of the "fun" of *Megatrends* is gone from the latest book, as the authors get down to the more serious business of re-inventing the corporation to fit the future they exclaimed over in that earlier attention-getting publication. Here they are specific with their advice, or options; they are opinionated but not pushy. Overall, **Re-inventing** still makes for pleasant and stimulating reading.

Content

BBR readers should be aware that many social thinkers consider Naisbitt and Aburdene's work too superficial and too optimistic. People also look with suspicion at the scope and tone of the authors' pretentions (blithely re-inventing the whole world) and at their enormous commercial success. Economists, journalists, and social scientists who labor in relative poverty and anonymity creating very complicated analyses of the human environment are naturally apt to be a bit resentful.

They may also have a legitimate point. One should be careful, therefore, about swallowing the authors' vision of the future whole. That does not mean, however, that there is not a lot of nourishment in **Re-inventing**. It seems to us that readers might well be able to divorce the practical, specific, and well-grounded advice (or what the authors call options for action) from the more cosmic and speculative projections.

Nor are the premises upon which the book is based hopelessly shaky. One may argue the timing and implications of the demographics, but the general trends are solid. And, granted their premises, Naisbitt and Aburdene's arguments are intellectually consistent.

What then do we gain from **Re-inventing the Corporation**? First, we see a refocus on the big picture. The authors make us step back and take the long view—an often invigorating, frequently valuable, and sadly neglected exercise. Second, several chapters offer some very good discussions of important topics: flexible work schedules, education and training, women in the work force, and health care costs. Many ideas of merit are there for the taking.

Reading Suggestions

There is no reason not to let yourself enjoy Naisbitt and Aburdene's presentation of the possibilities for the re-invented corporation. We suspect sound business people are not as likely to be swept away by rosy enthusiasm as some social commentators apparently fear. Turn your hard critical eye on the book's more sweeping projections and leave your mind open to the possibilities.

Ordering Information:	Warner Books 666 Fifth Avenue New York, New York 10103
Call:	(212) 484-2900
Specify:	ISBN 0-446-51284-2
Price:	$17.50

Competitive Advantage: Creating and Sustaining Superior Performance

Michael E. Porter

Free Press

© 1985
557 pages

Evaluation: A very impressive, comprehensive, and detailed volume that provides both the conceptual framework and the practical advice needed to create and sustain a competitive advantage. Designed as a complement to an earlier book on competitive strategy, it will, nonetheless, stand alone for readers with sufficient experience.

Thesis: By understanding and systematically applying the principles of competitive advantage and building on the concepts of competitive strategy, a firm can establish a long-term record of superior performance.

Audience: Specifically designed for practitioners responsible for their firm's strategic planning; also for managers and scholars who wish to increase their understanding of competitive strategy.

Reading Time: 15 to 18 hours; see Reading Suggestions for the team approach.

Author

Michael E. Porter teaches competitive strategy at Harvard Business School. He is also a guest columnist for *The Wall Street Journal* and a consultant.

Audience and Intentions

Porter's premise is that "competitive advantage is at the heart of a firm's performance in competitive markets." He feels that this is increasingly true as world economic growth slows and global competition intensifies. Porter also believes that the competitive *strategies* of many firms fail because they have not been translated "into the specific action steps required to gain competitive *advantage*" (emphasis added).

Consequently, the purpose of this book is to "build a bridge between strategy formulation and implementation." Specifically, it is designed to show "how a firm can actually create and sustain a competitive advantage in its industry—how it can implement the broad generic strategies." It is also intended to cut across the disciplines of marketing, production, finance, and others to present a "holistic view." Porter thus hopes to offer a comprehensive and practical volume that is beyond the scope of the current literature.

Porter says that he writes for "practitioners who are responsible for a firm's strategy and must decide how to gain competitive advantage." Because "potential sources of competitive advantage are everywhere in a firm," the book is also for "employees" at any level. It is, of course, also for "scholars" doing conceptual research.

Competitive Advantage builds upon the framework constructed in Porter's earlier book, *Competitive Strategy* (Free Press, 1980). The second book assumes "an understanding of industry structure and competitor behavior," which was the subject of the first work. Porter's "bridge between strategy formulation and implementation" is built in chapter 1, where he presents the core concepts of competitive strategy and links these concepts to the principles of competitive advantage defined in chapter 2.

The remaining chapters deal with aspects of implementation. Because the book is so vast and detailed, and because chapters 1 and 2 are so central to an understanding of the author's perspective, the Summary below will concentrate most heavily on the first two chapters.

Summary

Chapter 1: Competitive Strategy: The Core Concepts
(30 pages)

The aim of competitive strategy is to establish a profitable and sustainable position against the forces that determine industry competition. Choosing a strategic option entails analyzing both the attractiveness of the industry for long-term profitability and the relative competitive positions within the industry.

The five competitive forces that determine industry profitability are (1) the entry of new competitors, (2) the threat of substitutes, (3) the bargaining power of buyers, (4) the bargaining power of suppliers, and (5) the rivalry of existing competitors. The strength of each is a function of industry structure—that is, the industry's underlying economic and technical characteristics. Industry structure influences prices, costs, supply and demand, and level of investment.

A firm's position in the industry is the second factor determining its sustainable competitive advantage. The two basic types of competitive advantage—low cost and differentiation—lead to three generic strategies for above average performance in an industry: cost leadership, differentiation, and focus (either cost or differentiation). The first two seek a broad range of industry segments; the focus alternatives aim at a narrow segment.

A firm that engages in each generic strategy but fails to achieve any of them is "stuck in the middle" with no competitive advantage. Under most conditions, firms must make a choice. Choices involve tradeoffs and risks; they also need to be revised as the industry evolves for competitive advantage to be sustained.

Part I: Principles of Competitive Advantage

Chapter 2: The Value Chain and Competitive Advantage
(29 pages)

The value chain is a basic tool for analyzing the sources of competitive advantage. It breaks a firm down into strategically relevant activities in order to reveal the behavior of costs and the existing and potential sources of differentiation.

Value is the amount buyers are willing to pay for what a firm provides. The value chain consists of value activities and margin (see figure). Activities are either primary—involved in the physical creation of the product, its sale, transfer, and service—or support. Primary activities include inbound logistics (receiving and storing), operations, outbound logistics (distributing), marketing and sales, and service. Support activities include procurement, technology development (improvement of product and process), human resource management, and firm infrastructure (general management, planning, finance, etc.).

Within each category of primary and support activities, there are three types: (1) direct activities, which create value for the

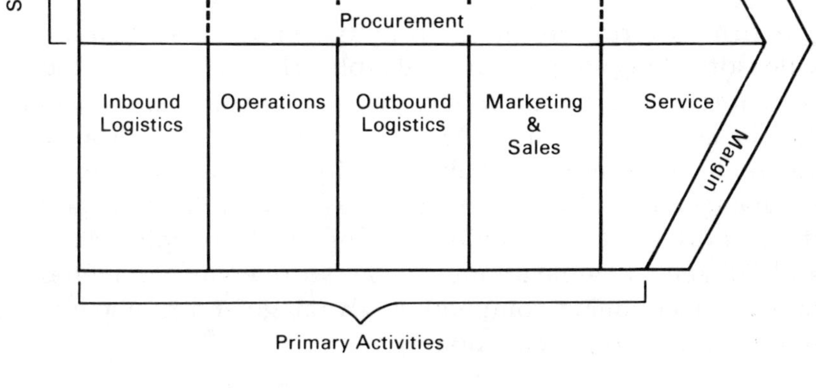

buyer; (2) indirect activities, which sustain direct activities, and (3) quality assurance. All activities are interdependent; their linkages can lead to competitive advantages. Vertical linkages also exist between a firm's value chain and the value chains of suppliers, channels, and buyers in a value system.

The value chain can also be used to design organizational structure by examining how the activities in a firm are and could be grouped. An organizational structure that corresponds to the value chain will improve a firm's ability to create and sustain competitive advantage.

Chapter 3: Cost Advantage (57 pages)

Since the behavior of a firm's costs stems from the value activities, cost analysis should examine costs within these activities and not the costs of the firm as a whole. Cost advantage results when the firm achieves a lower cumulative cost of performing value activities than its competitors.

Cost leadership is achieved by controlling the 10 major "cost drivers" that are the structural causes of the cost of an activity: economies of scale, learning, capacity utilization, linkages, interrelationships, integration, timing, discretionary policies, location, and institutional factors. For long-term success, a firm must sustain the cost advantage and avoid the pitfalls in a leadership strategy.

Chapter 4: Differentiation (45 pages)

A firm differentiates itself from its competitors when it provides something unique that is valuable to buyers. Differentiation is characterized by premium pricing, greater sales volume, and/or customer loyalty. Differentiation grows out of a firm's value chain because any value activity is a potential source of uniqueness. The "drivers of uniqueness" are roughly analogous to the cost drivers, the most important of which are policy changes and linkages. Examination of a firm's drivers of uniqueness is critical to sustaining competitive advantage and to uncovering new sources of differentiation.

Firms should also keep in mind that differentiation is costly and, to be useful, must create value for buyers. Uniqueness can be enhanced by strategic actions, but firms must also be aware of the pitfalls to differentiation.

Chapter 5: Technology and Competitive Advantages

(37 pages)

A technology is important for competition if it significantly affects a firm's competitive advantage or industry structure. Because technology is embedded in every value activity, the firm's value chain can be used to understand the role of technology in competitive advantage. Technological change is desirable if it lowers costs or enhances differentiation and if the firm's technological lead is sustainable—or if it improves overall industry structure.

Technology strategy attempts to turn technology into a competitive weapon. Strategy formulation is a seven-step process, in which management must (1) identify all the distinct technologies in the value chain, (2) identify potentially relevant technologies in other industries, (3) determine the likely path of change, (4) determine what changes have potential strategic significance, (5) assess the firm's relative capabilities, (6) select a strategy that reinforces the firm's overall competitive strategy, and (7) reinforce business unit technology strategies at the corporate level.

Chapter 6: Competitor Selection (28 pages)

The right competitors can strengthen rather than weaken a firm's competitive position in many industries. The strategic benefits of "good" competitors include (1) increasing competitive advantage, (2) improving current industry structure, (3) aiding market development, and (4) deterring entry of "bad" competitors.

Diagnosing a competitor's goals, assumptions, strategy, and capabilities will reveal whether it is beneficial or harmful to your position. There are also techniques for influencing the pattern of competitors by attacking some but not others. The goal is to obtain the optimum market share, which is rarely 100 percent. Once again, however, firms must be aware of the pitfalls in competitor selection.

Part II: Competitive Scope within an Industry

Chapter 7: Industry Segmentation and Competitive Advantage (42 pages)

Segments of an industry differ in their structural attractiveness and in the requirements for competitive advantage. Firms must determine in what segments focus strategies will be sustainable. The value chain can be used to diagnose differences in product varieties or buyers that lead to industry segmentation. The industry segmentation matrix is then employed to describe the overall picture of the industry.

At this point, a firm can adopt a broadly targeted strategy that addresses many segments or a focus strategy that addresses a small number of segments. Firms must analyze the attractiveness of the individual segments and their interrelationships. They must also not lose sight of the goal of sustainability for the competitive advantages they seek.

Chapter 8: Substitution (42 pages)

Substitution is the process by which one product or service supplants another; it is one of the five competitive forces determining the profitability of an industry. Substitution analysis is the method used to decide how best to defend against a substitute or how best to promote substitution as an offensive strategy.

The first step is the deceptively complex task of identifying the substitutes an industry faces. Next comes the examination of the three factors constituting the economics of substitution: (1) the relative value/price of a substitute compared to an industry's product, (2) the cost of switching, and (3) the buyer's propensity to switch. The firm can then adopt an offensive or defensive strategy designed to promote or inhibit substitution, respectively, keeping in mind that these factors change over time.

Part III: Corporate Strategy and Competitive Advantage

Chapter 9: Interrelationships among Business Units
(47 pages)

Horizontal strategy is a coordinated set of goals and policies across distinct but interrelated business units designed to enhance competitive advantage of the units and the corporation as a whole. Horizontal strategy continues to grow in importance because interrelationships are increasing in importance.

The three broad types of interrelationships among business units are tangible, intangible, and competitor. They can all be analyzed by the value chain in terms of forms of sharing, potential competitive advantages, and most likely sources of compromise cost. All play a role in horizontal strategy.

Chapter 10: Horizontal Strategy (19 pages)

Horizontal strategy must be explicit rather than implicit so that business units will not act against the larger interests of the corporation. Formulating horizontal strategy follows the seven-step process of (1) identifying all tangible interrelationships, (2) tracing tangible interrelationships outside the firm, (3) identifying possible intangible interrelationships, (4) identifying competitor interrelationships, (5) assessing the importance of interrelationships to competitive advantage, (6) developing a coordinated horizon strategy to enhance the most important relationships, and (7) creating horizontal organizational mechanisms to ensure implementation.

Chapter 11: Achieving Interrelationships (33 pages)

Achieving interrelationships is difficult for many firms because of a variety of impediments that can raise costs. These include (1) unequal benefits to different business units, (2) loss of autonomy and control, (3) biased incentive systems, (4) differing business unit circumstances, (5) fear of tampering with decentralization, and (6) a sense of unfairness.

Impediments can be overcome with such organizational mechanisms as horizontal structure, systems, human resource practices, and conflict resolution processes. These sometimes temporary devices cut across business unit lines to encourage managers to pursue interrelationships. The mechanisms are given life by shared values.

Chapter 12: Complementary Products and Competitive Advantage (27 pages)

Complementary products, such as computer hardware and software, are used jointly by the buyer. When an industry's products employ complements, one strategic option is to control them at the source by offering a full range of products. Advantages come from an improved perception of value by the buyer, differentiation, reduced costs, and optimal pricing.

A second option is bundling: selling a group of distinct but complementary products together only as a bundle at a single price. Bundling can entail risks, but does offer the possibility of lowered costs and increased differentiation.

A third option is cross-subsidization, which is selling one product at terms that deliberately promote the sale of complementary products. "Loss leader" and "trade-up" strategies apply this option.

Part IV: Implications for Offensive and Defensive Competitive Strategy

Chapter 13: Industry Scenarios and Competitive Strategy under Uncertainty (37 pages)

A scenario is an internally consistent projection of the future. Industry scenarios are increasingly being used to address the strategic implications of uncertainty. A set of plausible scenarios can help in the design of a competitive strategy: the procedure is (1) to identify the uncertainties that may affect industry structure, (2) to determine the causal factors driving them, (3) to make a range of plausible assumptions about each important causal factor, (4) to combine assumptions into internally consistent scenarios, (5) to analyze the industry structure that would prevail under each scenario, (6) to determine the sources of competitive advantage under each scenario, and (7) to predict competitor behavior under each scenario.

Chapter 14: Defensive Strategy (31 pages)

Defensive strategy aims to repel attacks by challengers, whether they are new entrants into the industry or established competitors. Assaults come in stages, so firms must evaluate the entire attack not just the first wave. The basic tactics underlying a defensive strategy are (1) raising structural barriers, (2) increasing expected retaliation against the challenger, and (3) lowering the inducement for an attack. Defensive tactics should be evaluated in terms of their value to buyers, costs, and sustainability. Defensive strategies are of two types: (1) deterrence and (2) response. Both attempt to alter a challenger's assessment of the attractiveness of a move against the defending firm.

Chapter 15: Attacking an Industry Leader (24 pages)

Leaders should *not* be attacked head on with an imitative strategy. To launch a successful attack against a leader, a challenger must (1) possess a clear and sustainable advantage in either cost or differentiation, (2) have some way of partly or wholly neutralizing the leader's advantage, and (3) be able to blunt the leader's retaliation.

Avenues for attack include reconfiguration of the entire value chain (as with product or market changes), redefinition of competitive scope, or purchase of market position through superior resources. Leaders display signs of possible vulnerability when they are stuck in the middle between generic strategies, have unhappy buyers, or are encountering regulatory problems. Industry signals of possible leader vulnerability consist of changes in technology, buyers, input costs, and distribution channels. An attack on a leader is unwise, however, if it destroys industry structure.

* * *

The book contains a short bibliography, no chapter source notes, and an index.

Evaluation

Presentation

Porter has done an impressively professional job of presenting a complicated technical construct. There are simply no wasted words in 528 pages of text. The concepts are precisely argued; the examples are compact, concise, and to the point; the diagrams are illuminating and helpful. In short, **Competitive Advantage** offers the kind of educational experience that can best be appreciated by those who are actually battling the serious problems of the professional world.

Content

Porter's book seems to offer everything you need to know to create and sustain a competitive advantage, just as promised. Taken with his previous book, it may be all you need to formulate and implement a competitive strategy. This does not mean, however, that it does everything for you. Comprehensive and detailed, conceptual and practical though it may be, the book demands time and concentration to read and master. And when you've finished, you still have to "formulate and implement" your own strategy in your own particular environment. It is, in other words, the very antithesis of one-minute management.

Reading Suggestions

Competitive Advantage cannot be profitably digested over a weekend or during two or three business days. Porter apparently meant for this book—and its earlier companion—to reproduce the MBA courses on competitive strategy he developed for Harvard. Thus your best approach is probably to treat them as extended, serious projects for your strategic team. Get multiple copies or pass the book(s) around to a few key people. Have everyone read a chapter or a few at a time—do chapters 1 and 2 by themselves, then follow the part divisions of the book—and come together for scheduled periods of discussion. Assign a leader or presenter for each session. **Competitive Advantage** is well worth this sort of effort.

Ordering Information:	Free Press Macmillan Publishing Co. Front & Brown Street Riverside, NJ 08075
Call:	1-(800) 257-5755
Specify:	ISBN 0-02-925090-0
Price:	$23.95

The Management Challenge: Japanese Views

Lester C. Thurow, editor

The MIT Press

© 1985
237 pages

Evaluation: A collection of essays on the Japanese business experience by Japanese professionals and professors, each with commentary by the editor (a well-known liberal economist) that draws lessons for the U.S. economy. The book makes for very dry reading but offers valuable perspectives and insights—even for the strongly market-oriented reader.

Thesis: We cannot copy what the Japanese are doing, but we can learn from their experience and perhaps apply new ideas to a reblending of U.S. economic practices and institutions.

Audience: Decision makers and policy makers in the business community and government; concerned citizens.

Reading Time: 7 to 8 hours; some selective skimming could cut the time a little.

Editor and Contributors

Lester C. Thurow is the Gordon Y. Billard Professor of Economics and Management at the Sloan School of Management of The Massachusetts Institute of Technology. Dr. Thurow has won several awards as an economist and as a writer of economics. He is the author of *The Zero-Sum Society* (1980) and *Dangerous Currents* (1983).

The contributors are 11 Japanese professors, managers, and executives. They are profiled in some depth in the book.

Audience and Intentions

Professor Thurow begins his book with a very important history lesson. In the eighteenth and nineteenth centuries America narrowed the economic gap between itself and Great Britain (and the rest of Europe) by stealing European technology (U.S. history books say "copying") and using it to make either better or cheaper products. By 1900 we had caught up and had to do our own inventing, although most basic scientific breakthroughs were still made in Europe.

The destruction wrought by World War II helped give us a huge economic and technological lead over the rest of the world. Until the late 1970s, "America enjoyed effortless superiority." This leadership is now gone or greatly diminished, which is not necessarily a bad situation as long as we don't continue to slide (relative to other industrial nations) as Great Britain has done. To maintain our standing, we must therefore "reaccelerate our rate of productivity" in order to reach parity with the productivity growth of other nations, notably Japan.

"To meet this objective," Thurow believes "will require some fundamental rebuilding of American institutions and practice." Although "significant upgrading" will be needed in several areas, such as worker training and investments, this book "focuses primarily on the management component." The learning process will be the same used by Americans in previous centuries and by Japanese today: we will have to accumulate bits and pieces from the competition that can be used *or modified* to good effect.

Of course, many, many books have attempted to draw lessons from the Japanese—the main competition—over the past several years. What makes **The Management Challenge** distinctive is the inside perspective provided by Japanese academics and businessmen who contribute essays on management to this collection. Thurow concludes each chapter with a brief (two-page) commentary "analyzing some of the implications... for the reblending of the American economic mixture." The goal is "not to copy what the Japanese are doing but to use their experience as a source of new ideas."

The book concentrates on macro issues of national economic policy, which is not necessarily the same as government policy. Consequently, it is designed for leaders and decision makers in business and government—and citizens concerned with the economic future of the country.

Summary

Introduction (17 pages)

In his introduction to the collection, Thurow provides the historical perspective described above and comments on the Japanese and U.S. economies. He notes, for instance, that while we may not want the zero employee turnover of the Japanese system, we may have overemphasized personal mobility. Our seniority system protects the jobs of workers but does not provide the sense of economic security and mutual obligation that one finds in Japan. Yet economic security is what American workers want most. The Japanese seem to understand that cooperative management-labor relations are forged in good times, not with union "give-backs" obtained during economic unrest.

The investments of U.S. firms are pulled along by capital's search for a high rate of return. Japanese investments are pushed into areas that utilize the skills of the labor force. We might, Thurow suggests, opt for less efficiency in capital markets and more in labor markets. Our current focus is due to incentives that point managers toward the short-term gain. Japanese firms are also willing to accept a smaller rate of return—a factor every bit as important as their lower labor costs. Finally, the Japanese appear to be more aware of the evolving business environment, especially the need to be competitive in the international market. They will continue to adapt to the changing realities of the world, and so must we.

Chapter 1: Motivation and Productivity (13 pages)

Hiroshi Takeuchi, managing director of the Long-Term Credit Bank of Japan, explains that the principle of equality prevails in Japanese business. With no heroes or elite employees, most people are promoted simultaneously through the same route. Even drop-outs can be regenerated later. Productivity comes from a balance of competition and cooperation between employees. All supervisors from the CEO down listen to and take into consideration the opinions of their subordinates. Thus worker motivation is high as well.

Thurow comments that while it is impossible for America to copy the Japanese system of pay and employment, we can learn to "reblend our incentives" by putting more emphasis on creating a good team and less on promoting brilliant individuals on the fast track.

Chapter 2: The Impact of Japanese Culture on Management (11 pages)

Masakazu Yamazaki is a professor of theater at Osaka University. He says that Japan is culturally pluralistic because Western culture has been studied and accepted but not assimilated. It has led to "agnosticism without nihilism" and a rational pragmatism based on trial and error. "Most Japanese are ironical pessimists," but without "gloom." They have evolved an ethic of hard work, which makes them willing to pour all their energy into day-to-day business. People gain knowledge of themselves through deeds.

According to Thurow, "agnosticism without nihilism" means that the individual is open to change without "being locked into a specific framework that knows what is 'true'." He contrasts our pragmatism with our "crusading attitude" and our yearning for a golden economic past that never really existed.

Chapter 3: The Perceptions and the Reality of Japanese Industrial Relations (27 pages)

Haruo Shimada is a professor of economics at Keio University. He contends that the common perception of Japanese business practices as an extension of traditional culture is inaccurate and reflects lack of well-balanced and reliable information about Japanese industrial relations. Outsiders have tended to study large, successful companies in the private sector—and then only after the miraculous economic growth of the 1950s and 1960s. As a result, they have seen the finished product.

Shimada concludes that (1) Japanese management style is not synonymous with industrial success because many companies practice it and are not successful, and (2) the industrial growth of the country is the result of a long, painstaking process of social engineering.

Thurow believes the United States can restructure its economic system by creating the kind of crisis situation in which people are willing to make necessary sacrifices—as Japan did after defeat in World War II. He thinks we can bring back the American tradition of equality of opportunity in the workplace through participatory management practices that improve team spirit, tap ideas and talent, and reduce the "worker-versus-management class society."

Chapter 4: The Firm and the Market in Japan (13 pages)

Hiroyuki Itami, a professor at Hitotsubashi University, describes how the Japanese use a mixture of market and organizational principles to allocate resources. They are, for instance, less able to redistribute labor *across* firms according to market needs because of life-time employment practices, but more able to respond to an individual firm's internal labor market by moving employees *within* the company. There is more use of administrative guidance from government and banks and fewer levels of management through which to transmit decisions.

Thurow believes that we can learn from the Japanese to reevaluate the advantages of market and organizational principles. The market is not always better than the organization in a competitive world; sometimes government can "lubricate the system."

Chapter 5: The Japanese Financial System: Past, Present, and Future (21 pages)

Shoichi Royama, a professor of monetary theory at Osaka University, contends that the Japanese financial system is in a process of transition because of the growth of the economy and the increase of international competition. The postwar Japanese economy has been characterized by the dominance of banks and the artificially low interest rate policy that led to "overborrowing." The status quo was challenged by the serious inflation and oil crises of the 1970s. Responses included the development of a short-term money market and the expansion of bond markets. In the future, the Japanese financial system will become much more market oriented, although the transition will be slow and incremental.

Thurow contends that Japan's evolution toward a more market-oriented economy should *not* be read as a confirmation of the U.S. system. It should show us that new conditions require new responses. He believes, for example, that the U.S. economy now needs investment banks to complement venture capital as a source of long-term investment funds.

Chapter 6: Product Diversification (19 pages)

Ichiro Hattori is chairman of Epson Corporation and a director of overseas subsidiaries of Seiko. He explains that Japanese corporate diversification programs must be viewed in the context of Japanese management environment: company-based unions, lifetime employment, seniority promotions, and employees' sense of belonging to a corporate community. Corporate management has an obligation to make every employee aware of the changes in the environment that made it necessary for the firm to alter its course of operations. Managers must explain the strategic view in order to obtain the cooperation of subordinates and effectively mobilize company resources.

Thurow says that the Japanese approach of combining the general strategic view from management with the information available in the field is time consuming but ultimately more successful than restricting planning to the top. This second approach leads to mergers of unlikely companies and chases the mirage of quick success.

Chapter 7: Strategy for Overseas Markets (17 pages)

Takashi Kiuchi is the general manager of planning for the international division of Mitsubishi Electric. He believes that Japanese companies will increasingly move their overseas operations headquarters to foreign countries. To maintain economic growth, Japan will step up exports. The central problem will be to mitigate friction with other countries, without sacrificing the integrity of the Japanese social structure. In their overseas operations, Mitsubishi is striving to reduce friction by (1) relying as much as possible on local employees, (2) constructing plants where demand is high, and (3) cooperating with major companies abroad.

Thurow advises American firms wishing to export to develop a willingness to be patient and to study foreign markets to determine what foreigners want. Industrial leaders in the 1990s, he believes, will need a strong international base.

Chapter 8: Competition and Cooperation among Japanese Corporations (21 pages)

Munemichi Inoue is manager of economic research and information for the Marubeni Corporation. He contends that the driving forces for rapid growth in Japan have been (1) *competition* between firms for managerial and technological innovation and (2) *cooperation* between firms within industrial groups. These groups are similar to the prewar *zaibatsu*, but operate with more independence. They cooperate to import energy resources, introduce technology, and launch new businesses. However, changes in environmental conditions at home and abroad have fostered increased competition and decreased cooperation. The challenge to Japanese industry is to forge a new balance between these two forces.

Thurow reminds us that, when the United States had a huge economic and technological lead over the rest of the world, it was appropriate to restrict cooperation between firms. Today, however, competition from foreign sources necessitates greater cooperation in terms of relaxed antitrust laws and joint ventures in technological research.

Chapter 9: Japan's Industrial Policy (31 pages)

Toshimasa Tsuruta, a professor of economics at Senshu University, believes that, although the government has played a significant role in Japan's economic development, the concept of Japan, Inc., is too simplistic and misleading. The protectionist policies of postwar Japan were common for developing companies attempting to facilitate industrialization. The pattern since has been one of gradual decontrol.

Government intervention was successful in limiting competition in basic industries such as steel. On the other hand, MITI's failure to curb new entries in the auto industry demonstrated the limitations of administrative guidance. The trade and capital liberalization of the 1960s completely destroyed Japan, Inc., and Japan's antimonopoly policy has been gradually strengthened. Today, Japan is facing the problems of a mature economy and must adapt with new policies.

Thurow defines the goal of industrial policy as linking the virtues of planning with the virtues of the market, of having decentralization and coordinated strategic planning where each is useful. Planning is appropriate when both the public and private sectors approve of a project, such as fifth-generation computer research, before it is undertaken.

Chapter 10: Economic Planning in Japan (27 pages)

Saburo Okita is an advisor to the government on economic planning and international policy. Dr. Okita contends that the Japanese economy is basically a highly competitive market economy. Direct intervention by the government in private industry has declined to the point of near nonexistence. Conversely, the government is increasing its responsibilities for improving social conditions and preventing serious business fluctuations.

In Japan, however, the usefulness of planning is still recognized. It helps individuals and enterprises evaluate macroeconomic changes. It focuses on balanced growth and long-term policy. Planning takes into account the slowing of Japan's economic growth and the change in relationship between Japan and the world economy. Japan will have to deal with three major currents of change: internationalization, an aging population, and economic maturity.

Thurow believes that America needs a "new grand design geared to the next century." We could do worse than adopt some Japanese strategic objectives: develop a system in tune with the new age, a good social infrastructure, and sound international relations.

Chapter 11: The Japanese Economy: Present and Future
(13 pages)

Hisao Kanamori is head of the Japan Economic Research Center. His analysis indicates that Japan's rapid growth in the 1960s was due to (1) an increase in capital from a high rate of savings, (2) a rise in productivity from a high rate of innovation, and (3) a growth in consumer demand in both domestic and foreign markets. The comparatively low growth in the 1970s may have been tied to a decline in Japan's growth potential and/or to the oil crises. If Japan makes some structural reforms and stimulates demand, its economy could grow 4 percent annually for the remainder of the century.

Thurow's comments focus on the elements of Japanese success. He considers the most important elements to be the implementation of social and economic innovation, the building of consensus, and the minimization of conflicts between the economy as a whole and individuals.

° ° °

The book has an index but no bibliography or footnotes.

Evaluation

Presentation

Each of the 11 essays by a Japanese business professional or professor ends with a two-page commentary by Thurow. His contributions are very well crafted. They efficiently pick up the themes of the essays and relate the significance of the Japanese experience to U.S. concerns. Unfortunately, because the commentaries are so brief, we are given opinions, in context, rather than developed arguments.

Thurow's commentaries are not executive summaries; you have to read the whole chapter to supply the background. Surprisingly, the Japanese essays are not always well focused, and only about one-half contain a "conclusion" section. The style tends to be mechanical, businesslike, and dry.

Content

Collections of essays always present a problem of focus. No matter how well the contributors are selected or how well the results are edited, the final product will not produce a coherent theme. **The Management Challenge** might have profited, therefore, from a final chapter by Thurow in which conclusions were drawn based on his chapter commentaries. The introduction to the essays is of some help in this regard, but falls short of providing a truly unifying theme.

The collection format is, however, revealing in two respects. First, the different points of view are very illuminating. It is instructive, for instance, to note how the Japanese experts disagree about the relationship of Japanese history and cultural tradition to their successful business practices. Second, the material that is repeated from essay to essay helps indicate what can most safely be considered reliable and widely held Japanese views.

Despite the view of some insiders who focus on the differences between Japanese firms or industries, there still appears to be a consensus on the similarities that define Japanese management. These include (1) a climate of corporate responsibility for the creation and maintenance of employment, (2) company-based unions, (3) lifetime employment, (4) seniority-based wages and promotions, (5) employees' sense of belonging to a corporate community.

It is important to reemphasize that Thurow does not believe we should copy these Japanese elements in America. He does believe we must "reblend the economic mix," taking advantage of what we can learn from our most successful global competitors. It should be noted that, in expounding his new "economic mix," Thurow reveals his interventionist proclivities. For example, he believes that a successful industrial policy requires "discretion," while "...the American tradition is one of giving government officials little discretion. They are boxed in with rules and regulations to ensure that they are fair and do not abuse their power." Even for readers who would prefer government officials to *remain* "boxed in," however, the variety of perceptions offered in **The Management Challenge**, along with the sundry Japanese points of view are sufficiently valuable to merit the consideration of economic decision makers.

The book also provides a valuable historical perspective on the evolving economic status of the United States—and other nations—provided by Thurow and by several of the contributors. It is astonishing how often we—experienced and informed as we may be—need reminders that the fortunes of nations are fluid. No natural law ordains superiority or prosperity for anyone. The message of **The Management Challenge**, therefore, is to keep learning and remain open to change.

Reading Suggestions

Begin your reading with Thurow's introduction. Some of the essays can be effectively skimmed, but don't skip them completely or Thurow's commentaries will lose their context. Conclude by rereading the introduction.

Ordering Information: The MIT Press
28 Carleton Street
Cambridge, Massachusetts 02142

Call: (617) 253-2884

Specify: ISBN 0-262-20053-8

Price: $14.95

The Knowledge Executive

Harlan Cleveland

Truman Talley Books
E.P. Dutton

© 1985
261 pages

Evaluation: An intellectually stimulating book about an important issue: the need for well-rounded leaders in an era of specialization. The author examines the revolutionary changes brought about by the marriage of computers and telecommunications and suggests what qualities we must now look for in our leaders.

Thesis: Information has become our chief resource, and this is changing all the old management ground rules. Now, we need generalist leaders who will rule, not by fiat, but by consensus, and who will always keep one eye on the big picture.

Audience: Decision makers and policy makers in all private businesses and public institutions; anyone interested in societal trends. The book is accessible to all intelligent readers.

Reading Time: 6 to 8 hours.

Author:

Harlan Cleveland has been editor and publisher of *The Reporter*, assistant secretary of state for international organization affairs, U.S. ambassador to NATO, and president of the University of Hawaii. Current, he is a professor and dean of the Hubert H. Humphrey Institute of Public Affairs at the University of Minnesota. Cleveland has written several books, including *The Future Executive: A Guide for Tomorrow's Managers.*

Audience and Intentions:

According to Cleveland, we are "living at the confluence of more historic transitions at once than any of our ancestors." Chief among these transitions is what Cleveland calls "the informatization of society," which has brought "a sudden increase in humanity's power to think, and therefore to organize." The informatization of society has been greatly accelerated in the 1980s by "the marriage of computers and telecommunications," so that information has come "to be regarded as a resource in itself."

So much information at our easy disposal encourages specialization, and this has left modern executives with the unenviable job of "managing more while understanding less." Consequently, there's a need for a "get-it-all-together profession," a class of leaders whose "indispensable quality of executive leadership is breadth."

In **The Knowledge Executive,** Cleveland intends first to show how the new information society has changed the old ground rules. Second, he expects to prove that we need broad-minded, generalist ("get-it-all-together people") leaders to guide us through the new knowledge environment. Finally, he hopes to show how we might cultivate this kind of leader and what kind of qualities we should be looking for. **The Knowledge Executive,** then, is a call for a new definition of leadership appropriate to a new environment.

Summary

Chapter 1: The Get-It-All-Together Profession (18 pages)

There was a time when leaders "led," when the educated and affluent few passed its decisions down to the complacent many. That arrangement, for better or worse, is gone. It has been replaced by a new horizontal society, a result of the modernizing effects of science and the Industrial Revolution. Today, people are rewarded for what they do instead of who they are; but what they do, increasingly, is organize themselves into specialties. Those specialists who achieve positions of executive leadership, however, must develop the aptitudes and attitudes of the generalist.

Generalists are skeptical of inherited assumptions, curious about the effects and benefits of technology, concerned about fairness, willing to take chances, and broad minded. It's important, also, that they be former specialists, since this allows them to judge the work of other specialists more accurately. Generalists are marked by "their concern for the general outcome"; they're get-it-all-together people.

Chapter 2: The Knowledge Dynamic (17 pages)

Information is no longer industry's mere handmaiden, but a resource all by itself. In fact, it has become our key resource, since it is so much more accessible than other resources. We must realize that information is not like other resources. It cannot, for instance, be grasped with metaphors borrowed from physics. Unlike other resources, information cannot be "used up." The ultimate effect of all knowledge is to arrange people or things in new ways. The method of delivering information (say, a book) and the information itself (what the book is about) are distinct entities.

An increasingly large proportion of our employment force is devoted to information work. The "service" sector soaks up three-fourths of our human resources, and more than two-thirds of this sector consists of information workers. Consequently, we must keep in mind that it is expandable, compressible, substitutable, transportable, shareable, and diffusive.

Chapter 3: The Twilight of Hierarchy (14 pages)

In the new knowledge environment, we have to rethink the very nature of rule, power, and authority. Information has traditionally offered an advantage to its bearer, but the nature of that advantage has changed. Today, leadership is based on persuasion and consensus, not command and control. In other words, authority is delegated upward, with most societal trends originating among the masses and only later receiving official confirmation. The task of leadership today is to help the followers go where they want to go.

Chapter 4: Costs and Benefits of Openness (22 pages)

The modern executive's most puzzling problem is: How do you get everybody in on the act and still get some action? Openness is the buzzword of modernization, universally praised; but how much openness is enough? Openness not only stops bad things (Nixon's dirty tricks, for instance), it can also prevent good things from happening. An inventory of the costs of openness would surely include: a tendency toward oversimplification and confrontation, apathy and nonparticipation, too much legalistic rule writing, too many public hearings, an excess of voting and parliamentary process, the protection of mediocrity, and difficulty in recruiting and evaluating job candidates. Openness is valued by everyone, but it must content with equally important principles: a person's right of privacy and the public's right to be served effectively by its public organizations.

Chapter 5: Ownership: Knowledge as a Shared Resource (14 pages)

Information is a "sharing resource," which means it cannot be effectively monopolized in the same way "real" resources can. Information is also a porous resource; any effort to contain it by technological fix is soon thwarted by a new technological antifix.

The distinction between the private and public sectors of the American economy is increasingly blurred. The federal government farms out to private companies everything from weapons production to health care. Conversely, large private corporations turn to the federal government for bailouts when they cannot meet their financial obligations. This creative mixture of private enterprise and public authority has made the United States a great country.

Chapter 6: Privilege: The Fairness Revolution (17 pages)

Theoretically, information-as-a-resource encourages two important developments: (1) the spread of benefits, rather than the concentration of wealth, and (2) the maximization of choice, rather than the suppression of diversity. Though minorities and women have made great strides in the United States, continued progress depends on the availability of education. Meanwhile, the very nature of information—its porousness, its expansiveness, its shareability—is helping to bring about a global fairness revolution, a rejection of the old alignments and concepts (property rights, etc.) by those who think markets are unjustly rigged in favor of the already favored. Only societies flexible enough to adapt to this pressure will be able to maintain a semblance of peace.

On the bright side, the fusion of computers and communications may well further the empowerment of the many, especially if there is sufficient access to education. Japan and South Korea are clear examples of countries whose economies have thrived despite limited natural resources. These countries have successfully exploited the only sure resource they have: the minds of their people.

Chapter 7: Geopolitics: The Passing of Remoteness (19 pages)

The informatization of society (a phrase that sounds better in its original French) is eroding hierarchies based on control, secrecy, ownership, and limited access to resources. It is also eroding power based on location. This is a change from the days when a country's importance was based on the natural resources contained within its borders. Today, civilizations are increasingly built around communities of people, not place. Consequently, interdependence is the order of the day, and the United States, which is perhaps the least remote country in the world, can help the rest of the world adapt to such mutual dependencies.

Chapter 8: The Social Fallout of Knowledge (20 pages)

Our basic ideas about societal issues seem to be lengthening to take in more of the future and widening to include what once were regarded as externalities. That is, societies have begun to realize that there are consequences to their decisions and actions. An example of narrower thinking in earlier days would be the Manhattan Project, which built the world's first atomic bomb. No one was hired onto the Manhattan Project to consider the social implications of the bomb's unprecedented power.

In the 1970s, however, society started to take charge, not of scientific discovery but of its technological fallout. The possible consequences of genetic research, for instance, have been widely discussed and debated.

Chapter 9: A Harness for Technology (14 pages)

As the rest of the world has been learning to develop its resources, the United States has been moving to a new stage of development that features the social assessment of new technologies even before they are deployed. Much of the impetus for this stems from the environmental movement, particularly the National Environmental Policy Act, which created the Environmental Impact Statement, a tool useful to opponents of technological change. A restrained approach to technological development was evidenced during the 1970s by the U.S. Senate's decision not to deploy the supersonic airplane and the nuclear power industry's failure to win general public support.

A new concern about human development and personal awareness has replaced the old desire for an endless stream of material goods. At the same time, people are turning to "experts on experts," who can guide them through technological change and direct that change toward human ends. This kind of get-it-all-together thinking is called technology assessment; it has practitioners both within government and in the private sector. Technology assessment is not meant to replace the old criteria of economic and social decision making—cost effectiveness, profitability, etc.—but simply to supplement those criteria with judgments about the direction of technological advance.

Chapter 10: The Generalist Mind-Set (23 pages)

A get-it-all-together person likes to work hard, enjoys using her or his mind, listens well, is always optimistic, and doesn't mind making difficult decisions. In the new knowledge environment, the get-it-all-together person should also be interested in what makes people tick, intellectually curious, unafraid of risks or newness, and willing to reconcile personal power with the responsibility that power entails.

The mind has a need to know and also a need not to know. Without the need not to know, we would all be awash in a sea of useless information. But the need not to know should never be used as an excuse to avoid responsibility.

Chapter 11: Education for Leadership (24 pages)

Automatic systems are replacing the jobs that many high school graduates used to perform; the jobs that are left will require education beyond the secondary level. In the new knowledge-rich society, different kinds of jobs will appear. Most of them will require more brainwork, more computer literacy, less competition, and continuing education. More and more people will work at the management of international interdependence, either in public or private organizations.

Two predictions about the future job market can be safely made. One, those persons who do not educate (and re-educate) themselves to participate in the knowledge environment will become the peasants of the information society. Two, those countries that fail to provide a relevant education for all their members will be left behind. In the United States and elsewhere, this will require a university-based fusion of integrative policy analysis, midcareer education for leadership, and the training of younger students for roles in the policy process. To accomplish this, we must favor an interdisciplinary approach over the customary division of knowledge into manageable compartments.

Chapter 12: The Knowledge Seniors: Commencement at 65 (12 pages)

As the by-product of a busy, productive, relevant life, leisure is a boon and a balm. As a purpose of life, it is a bust. Therefore, we shouldn't automatically turn out to pasture those workers who happen to reach an arbitrarily set age barrier—especially since those are often the very people who are most likely to have seen more of the world, mastered or at least dabbled in more specialties, and taken the time for reflection. In other words, mature and experienced people often have the best generalist credentials.

Afterword (5 pages)

Cleveland captures what he has learned in four decades of public and private management in a list of "fourteen aphorisms from experience."

* * *

There is an extensive Notes section that cites sources and additional reading material, with occasional elaboration on points made in the text. As is becoming the norm in professional literature, these citations have no identifying footnote or page numbers. The book also includes a detailed index.

Evaluation

Presentation

Cleveland manages—most of the time—the difficult task of being erudite without being pedantic. He is a widely experienced and learned man who writes in a learned style of a kind that, luckily, more often stimulates than irritates the intellect. He quotes extensively from politicians, poets, and philosophers, not all of whom would be known to even a well-educated reader. **The Knowledge Executive** is a reflective book by someone who enjoys listening to himself philosophize.

That is not to say, however, that Cleveland is completely self-indulgent. He has a very fluid, polished prose style and presents his arguments clearly, naturally, and pleasantly. His illustrations are from his personal experience, but they are generalizable and pertinent to the discussion. His humor has a quality of being pleased with itself, but we can readily share the jokes.

Content

As evident from the discussion above, **The Knowledge Executive** is a book of ideas. The dust jacket quotes John W. Gardner (a hero of Cleveland's) to the effect that this is a "profound how-to book." We might be willing to grant the profundity but hedge on the how-to. Abstraction certainly dominates practice here.

What might be considered the work's tangible contribution is Cleveland's lucid explanation of the changes wrought by the rising flood of computer-stored information. Chapters 2–7 explore the specific impacts of technological advance.

The prevailing value of the book, however, is the introduction of the concept of the "generalist" arising as the requisite manager of the future. Cleveland makes a good case for the imminent need for the well-rounded, far-sighted, ecological leader who has grown beyond specialist training.

Even here, however, the focus is on attitudes more than skills. **The Knowledge Executive** promotes and embodies the idea of philosopher-manager—not as a mythical ideal, but as the only practical approach to getting things done in the information society. It is a book about generalists for generalists (and aspiring generalists) by a truly actualized generalist. As such, we recommend it to all readers of open and inquiring mind.

Reading Suggestions

This is one of those rare books in which the Foreword is worth reading because it so admirably sets the tone. Go on to chapter 1 and then, perhaps, skip to chapter 10 for the comprehensive definition of generalist. Chapter 2–7 are companions, as are chapters 8 and 9. Chapters 11 and 12 and the Afterword are somewhat tangential but still worth reading.

Ordering Information:	Truman Talley Books E.P. Dutton 2 Park Avenue New York, New York 10016
Call:	(212) 725-1818
Specify:	ISBN 0-525-24307-0
Price:	$18.95

What They Don't Teach You at Harvard Business School

Mark H. McCormack

Bantam Books

© 1984
256 pages

Evaluation: This is one of those books that should be required reading in every business school curriculum. It is both entertaining and informative, and while much has been written before on many of the subjects McCormack covers—time management, dressing for success, negotiation techniques—his liberal use of examples drawn from personal experience provides fresh insights and gives each topic new appeal.

Thesis: Business situations invariably come down to people situations. What the instructors at Harvard don't teach you is what they *can't* teach you: how to read people and how to use what is read to achieve success in business. That brand of knowledge comes only from experience.

Audience: Business executives on every level of the corporate ladder; men and women who own their own businesses or are thinking about starting one.

Reading Time: 4 to 5 hours.

Author

Mark H. McCormack is a lawyer and the founder of International Management Group (IMG), which represents sports celebrities as well as such diverse entities as Wimbledon, the National Football League and the Nobel Foundation. He has served as a consultant to more than fifty Fortune 500 companies and is a frequent lecturer in business schools throughout the U.S. McCormack never attended Harvard Business School, but the success of his company is the topic of a case study there.

Audience and Intentions

Mark McCormack will not make many friends in academia with this book. But making such friends does not appear to be the author's purpose.

In the preface to **What They Don't Teach You at Harvard Business School**, McCormack writes that, as an education, an MBA or an LLB is "at best a foundation and at worst a naive form of arrogance." The best lesson anyone can learn from business school, he contends, is an awareness of what it can't teach. Lessons about human nature and how it affects business situations can be derived only from experience. McCormack illustrates this thesis with examples drawn from his own personal experience. The overwhelming success of his company is positive proof that those theories work.

McCormack is a firm believer in what he likes to call "street smarts." And, with this book, he purports to fill the gaps between a business school education and the "street knowledge" he has gleaned from the day-to-day experience of running a business and managing people for over twenty years.

Much of what McCormack has to say has, in fact, been said before. Numerous books have been published on such subjects as managing time, dressing for business, and closing the sale. What makes this book different is the author's willingness to name names and to demonstrate by example. He describes how his theories have worked in particular situations and how they might have worked in others. The result is a book that is both human and exceedingly credible.

While much of what McCormack has to say is geared to the business owner and to those thinking about going into business for themselves, the author does make a special point of speaking to the concerns of the "company" man and woman. Chapter 4, for example, is entirely devoted to how McCormack's management theories might be applied in a corporate setting. The audience for this book is everyone in business.

Summary

What They Don't Teach You opens with a preface in which McCormack sets down the thesis described above. The 14 chapters are divided into three parts. Section I (Chapters 1–4) lays the foundation for McCormack's theories about using one's knowledge about people to achieve and retain success. Section II (Chapters 5–10) deals with sales and negotiation techniques. In Section III (Chapters 11–14) McCormack offers tips on running a business. The book closes with a brief epilogue in which McCormack likens business to a game and cautions against becoming too satisfied with one's own success.

Section I: People

Chapter 1: Reading People (22 pages)

Because business situations always come down to people situations, the more you know about a person and the sooner you know it, the more effective you can be in business. Learning to read people involves seven basic steps: (1) listen aggressively; (2) observe aggressively; (3) talk less; (4) take a second look at first impressions; (5) take time to use what you have learned; (6) be discreet; and (7) be detached.

Chapter 2: Creating Impressions (26 pages)

How people relate to you in business is based on the conscious and unconscious statements you make about yourself. The way you dress, speak on the phone, phrase a letter, or greet people all affect the impressions you make on others.

The subtlety of making impressions demands self-awareness—knowledge of the impression you create and of the impression you *want* to create. People will forgive all sorts of "out-of-character" behavior if their overall, lasting impression of you is favorable.

Chapter 3: Taking the Edge (11 pages)

Taking the edge is the gamesmanship of business. It involves taking what you know about others and what you have allowed them to know about you and using this information to tilt business situations to your advantage. In any business situation, there is an edge for the taking.

Chapter 4: Getting Ahead (24 pages)

In the corporate setting, people who merely work up to their capabilities don't become stars. Those who become stars combine their capabilities with other things—savvy, people sense, an understanding of how the game is played. They make it to the top because they are effective in selling their ideas inside as well as outside the company. They play by the rules and they aren't afraid to make mistakes.

Section II: Sales and Negotiation

Chapter 5: The Problems of Selling (5 pages)

Most people are born salesmen. Unconsciously, we all use such tried and true sales techniques as persuasion and negotiation. But upon entering the work world, where our sales abilities are formally judged for the first time, most of us respond by convincing ourselves we can't sell, don't know how to sell, or don't want to sell.

Chapter 6: Timing (14 pages)

Many ideas fail not because they are bad ideas or because they are poorly executed, but because the timing is wrong. Don't be too quick to write off a good idea. If you believe in an idea, present it again when the timing is right. Persistence almost always pays off.

Chapter 7: Silence (5 pages)

Silence is as important to sales as talk—and sometimes more so. Knowing when to remain silent can strongly influence the impression you make on others. Furthermore, it's impossible to get a commitment out of someone if that person can't get a word in edgewise.

Chapter 8: Marketability (16 pages)

Marketability is an important aspect of sales success. It involves looking beyond the obvious to perceive underlying motivation and to determine the reasons why someone does or does not care about a product. Knowing a product means understanding the idea behind it and the image it projects. If you can't be enthusiastic about it, no one else will be either.

Chapter 9: Stratagems (13 pages)

Just as there is a right time to make a sale, there is usually a right place as well. It may be over lunch, on the golf course, or any place where the buyer's guard is likely to be down. Other stratagems include these: sell defensively; divide and conquer; expose a buyer to a product and let the exposure speak for itself; show up on the buyer's doorstep; and sell one-to-one.

Chapter 10: Negotiating (16 pages)

Negotiation is the last step in an ongoing sales effort, the culmination of a process that has probably lasted several months. When the time comes to negotiate, consider such principles as: let the other guy go first; don't deal in round numbers; avoid showdowns; and sweeten a deal with the buyer's self-interest.

Section III: Running a Business

Chapter 11: Building a Business (13 pages)

Building a business involves listening to your own common sense, then taking the necessary steps to turn theories into reality. Some important considerations include: commit (early on) to quality; be smart enough to know when you're lucky; grow slowly; diversify your expertise and talent; hire the best to teach you what you don't know; look to world markets; charge for your expertise; and go into business for the long-term.

Chapter 12: Staying in Business (35 pages)

Building a business and running one involve totally different sets of problems. The biggest single problem of staying in business is that the very structures and systems created to make a business flow smoothly soon begin to stifle the momentum they were originally designed to help.

Don't fall into the trap of letting structures run the operation or allowing policies to stifle it. As the company grows, try to preserve the "small feeling" it had from the start. The initial anxiety of wondering if the company will be around in six months puts an edge on everything you do and creates the esprit among workers that companies so often lose as they grow. Learn to delegate, and hire people smarter than yourself.

Chapter 13: Getting Things Done (32 pages)

When asked to list their greatest frustrations, executives almost always put not having enough time at the top of the list. The solution to the time management problem lies in controlling your business day rather than having it control you.

Effective time management techniques include: doing the things everyone else has to do at the time when everyone else isn't doing them; establishing an individualized organization system; allocating blocks of time for appointments and meetings based on the personalities involved; using the telephone effectively (don't play telephone tag); learning when to say no; and becoming a more effective decision maker.

Chapter 14: For Entrepreneurs Only (13 pages)

Starting a business has become the new Great American Dream. But if you want to be in your own business solely because you dislike your present job or your boss, your chances of success are limited. Starting a business is a financial, professional, and emotional commitment. You must ask yourself some hard questions: What are the connections? Why won't it work? You should also start small, be flexible and use the fear of failure to your advantage.

* * *

As you might expect, the book has no references, bibliography, or index.

Evaluation

Presentation

Mark McCormack's style makes this book both unique and worth reading. His hard-hitting, no-nonsense manner of doing business is evident in the way he puts words on paper. The result is a book that is as pleasant to read as it is believable.

By virtue of his style, McCormack comes across as arrogant and more than a little pleased with himself and his accomplishments. (Ironically, he cautions against such an attitude in the epilogue to this book.) He drops names incessantly and makes no bones about the fact that he believes his way of doing business is the right way. Some readers may find these personality quirks irritating, but it appears that it is precisely his brashness that has helped McCormack succeed. Using the theories he advocates, McCormack has built a company he started with less than $1,000 into a multi-million dollar corporation. This seems reason enough to excuse the arrogance and dropping of a name or two.

The reader need not agree with McCormack's theories or approve of the way he does business to appreciate this book's format and style. **What They Don't Teach You** is a good read regardless.

Content

What They Don't Teach You might just as easily have been titled "Principles of Management," for these three words quite accurately describe the book's content. McCormack lays out a concise, workable plan for successful business management. Between the covers of this book is a wealth of information about time management, negotiation, hiring and firing, salesmanship, entrepreneurship, and marketing—none of it presented in the dry, lifeless rhetoric that so often characterizes books about management.

The stated purpose of **What They Don't Teach You** is to fill the void between what *is* taught by business schools and what *can be* learned through experience. By sharing the secrets of his own success, McCormack accomplishes that goal.

On occasion, however, McCormack seems to contradict his own theories. He notes, for example, that successful business management cannot be learned in the classroom. Yet in the next breath, he implies that it can be learned from a book—his book, of course. In another chapter, he makes a point about how business executives should avoid wasting one another's time telephoning simply to chat. Later on, however, he tells how important it is to check in with a client if for no other reason than to discuss the weekend golf game.

These apparent contradictions aside, McCormack has many worthwhile ideas about achieving and hanging on to success. Those in Washington who wish to do away with tax deductions for the "three martini lunch" would do well to read McCormack's evaluation of how important social occasions are to successful business dealings.

His theories about salesmanship provide excellent rebuttals to arguments from those who consider sales a dirty word. And for anyone who has even remotely considered starting a business, McCormack offers some of the best, most clear-cut advice around: "If you want to be in your own business because you are 'sick and tired of being told what to do,' because you want more 'freedom,' or because you are unappreciated or undervalued, forget it."

Reading Suggestions

What They Don't Teach You is not the kind of book one might call compelling. It can be read over a cup of coffee and set aside for a day or two without any loss of continuity or comprehension.

Within each chapter, the book is organized into a series of scenarios. Some are as long as a page, but frequently they are only a paragraph or two. Each consists of a management point illustrated by an example drawn from the author's experience. Although grouped together to illustrate a general subject such as getting ahead or building a business, each scenario is self-contained. Thus, starting and stopping within a chapter does not take away from either the understanding or the enjoyment of the book as a whole.

Ordering Information:	Bantam Books, Inc. 666 Fifth Avenue New York, NY 10103
Specify:	ISBN 0-553-05061-3
Price:	$15.95
